YOU CAN'T MAKE THIS UP

...

But
Jesus
Can

Peter D. Blackshaw

You Can't Make This Up—But Jesus Can!

First Printing

DEDICATION

No one succeeds alone.
I am grateful to all who contributed to this journey.

Jesus

My family, Nick, Mike, Kristen and Keri, Mike Z, Brett, Kristeen
and all the grandkids

Shelley and Owen, the right hand of the ministry

Greg & Paige

The Stantons and the Carters

The Waldrops

The Sosas

The Hamiltons & Hills

Curry Blake

Ted Stump

Richard Montecalvo Sr.

Joseph DeAngelo

Christian DeBrow

The Sanders

Ted Stump

The Maqsoods

The Hoods

The Hickory ARC/IHT Family

My RANT Family

CONTENTS

Prologue
LOVE WINS!

They overcame him by the blood of the Lamb,
and by the word of their testimony.

REVELATION 12:11 (KJV)

There is no such thing as an ordinary Christian. If you are a believer who has accepted the sacrifice of Jesus on the cross for your sins by asking Him into your heart, then you are anything but ordinary. Unfortunately, many people accept Christ but then fail to follow through. This book is being written, in part, for those of us who need to be reminded that our stories (testimonies) become powerful and truly extraordinary when we fully surrender our lives to the Lord. Jesus can bring meaning and purpose out of every life experience. In those moments of inner healing, our mistakes and missteps become stepping stones for others to find their way out of the dark into the light. That is the power of the blood of Christ and testimonies bearing His name.

Prepare to have your world rocked. If you believe the Bible is the Word of God, then I invite you to dive deep into key Scriptures such as, "The things I do, you will do also" John 14:12 and "the same spirit that raised Christ from the dead lives in you." Romans 6:10

The Bible says in 2 Peter 1:4 that we can partake of the Divine nature. Before you read any further, take a moment and let that sink in. Jesus is inviting every true believer to step into their God-given authority and begin to operate in alignment with the power of Holy Spirit. For many Christians that is a hard concept to grasp. Make no mistake. Think of the Biblical accounts of things Jesus did then picture yourself doing those things. The Scriptures say what they mean and mean what they say. That makes this invitation personal to you! As many modern denominations have moved toward teaching that miracles no longer occur, I challenge you to resist the temptation to settle for any theology which seems to water down what Jesus is clearly teaching. Scripture magnifies the reality that we are capable of walking in the same authority which Adam and Eve walked in before the fall in the garden. I personally find it impossible to twist these Scriptures into any other meaning. Yet in the US and other countries I have visited, I have not found this powerful teaching to be common in churches, Bible studies, or Sunday

Schools. Why does this great chasm exist between the truth and daily reality for so many modern-day Believers? I'll explain what I have come to believe.

God created the world and everything in it. Furthermore, He did it without our help. Mankind was not yet created when the rest of creation came into existence at the hand of the Creator. In the book of Job, it says, "Where were you when I laid the foundations of the world?" Job 38:4 simply states that the days of creation were completed without any outside help from any being other than God Himself.

This leaves us to ponder why God would choose to include us, thereby allowing us to be partakers and participants in all that He is and all that He does? The answer is both simple and profound. Love. Pure love. God is love and love demands inclusion, sharing, sacrifice, and a laying down of all things selfish. Love is not just something God does. Divine love is an intrinsic part of His nature. It is the essence of who He is. He cannot separate Himself from love.

This Divine love is at the core of why we were also created with free will. Love cannot exist in an environment where there is no choice to love. If there were no choice, we would be operating on instinct, just as you see in the animal kingdom. Birds fly south for the winter. Bees build hives and make honey. Turtles come ashore to lay their eggs and hatchlings scramble to the sea. It is programmed into their nature. While instinctive nature drives animal actions, human beings operate uniquely from a place of choice. This free will instilled in mankind by God places people at the height of all God has chosen to create. This attribute sets us apart from the rest of God's glorious creation.

It is a mystery and an honor to be created by God for His Divine purpose, and yet to walk in free will. It is not His will to control us like robots. He loved us enough to create us, then He allows us to choose whether we devote our lives to His service. He deserves our love, yet He will never demand it. Only a true father knows what it is like to love a child even while watching he or she wander lost in the world. Imagine how much more our perfect Heavenly Father longs for us to come home into His heart where He can reveal His greatest plan for our lives. Jesus invites His sons and daughters to do the same and greater works than He did. While many might think the greatest invitation is to be part of His miracles, the greatest miracle of all is that Jesus invites me to allow Him to transform my life to bear His family name. True love is devoted to seeing me become all that God envisioned when He created me. The same is true for you!

We get a glimpse of just how amazing this truth is by observing the relationship of parents with their children. Think like a parent, with me, for a moment. You can get your children to obey you because you have power over them. In most cases, the child's will bends to the will of the parent. It is a holy privilege to gently guide the actions of a child as he or she matures. But think about how satisfying is it when that child performs a task strictly of their own free will, simply because they know it will please you. You have taught them well. God holds all authority in Heaven and on earth, yet He refuses to manipulate our choices or our actions. When we, of our own free will, seek to serve and please Him, we gain a higher level of access to the Kingdom of God. If an earthly father is prompted to reward his child who obeys, how much more does God wish to reward His sons and daughters who follow Him out of love? The Father's heart melts when we respond to Him that way. This moves His heart to open Heaven over our lives. You may ask what I mean when I speak of an open Heaven. The treasures of Heaven are opened for us. A great example is found in Exodus 21:2 of the servant who is freed after six years of service. This Old Testament Scripture tells us that if his response to his freedom was, "I love my master. I don't want to be free and I want to stay with him and serve him" his master would bring him to the door, pierce his ear with an awl into the door as a sign of his voluntary commitment to remain in service to the good master.

It has been said that a person can only have one master. Before a person comes to know Jesus as Savior, that person is a slave to sin and death. Much like in the story of the freed servant in Deuteronomy 15:17, the simple act of receiving Jesus into our hearts frees us from the bondage of sin, thereby launching us into the place where we are free to choose a life of following Christ out of pure love.

Salvation is much like walking through a doorway into a whole new life. This is no ordinary door! Jesus is the door of the sheep. We come to the Father through Him. By placing our faith in Jesus, we are saying that we now wish to stay with Him forever. Going one step further, we are also saying that we are choosing to become set apart for His purposes out of free will. Jesus said, "My sheep know my voice and will not follow another." This is the declaration of a loving God who longs to have His sons and daughters choose a life with Him on their own.

For any person who chooses a life apart from Christ, there is a somber warning. Rejecting the God we were created to walk with for all of eternity leaves our soul subject to the assault of Satan. I belong to God, but if I refuse to offer my life to Him, the enemy is nearby with plans to highjack my destiny. Free will in the hands of our adversary is a dangerous thing. The devil's lies, along with people's belief in those lies, have caused much pain and destruction in this world. I am thankful that, in the end, love wins.

Introduction
HOW THIS BOOK NAMED ITSELF

God also bore witness by signs and wonders and
various miracles and by gifts of the Holy Spirit
distributed according to his will.

HEBREWS 2:4

As I prayed about the possibility of writing this book, I
asked myself if the world really needs another Christian
book. Bookstore shelves are full of theology, self-help,
and get-rich-quick with Jesus books. Why in the world
would I want to add to that collection? What do I have
to say that would be any different? Would one more
book on the shelf make a difference?

It occurred to me that out of all the books I've encountered, I've never seen a writing that specifically
deals with the subject I chose to cover in this book.
There are many topics covered in the world of Christian
writing. The best way I can convey my passion and purpose behind this writing is to look into God's Word.

Consider the following verses, "In that day many will say to me, 'Lord, Lord, did we not prophesy in your name, and cast out demons in your name, and do many mighty works in your name?' And then will I declare to them, 'I never knew you; depart from me, you workers of lawlessness.'" Matthew 7:22-23

You see, we can know about God and not actually know God. We can work His works outside of a relationship with Him; however, in Exodus 33:11 it says that God spoke to Moses face to face as a man speaks to a friend. Those who wish to minister the healing gifts to others need to first align their lives fully with Jesus. It is fraudulent to go about trying to behave like Jesus or have similar results if our hearts are not fully surrendered to Him. If I were to cash a check which belongs to someone else by signing my own name on it, I would be taking something that did not belong to me. That money belonged in someone else's hands. This is a good illustration of the inheritance that is held in trust for those who willingly love and serve God. The family name can then give access to all that is held in trust for those who love Jesus.

In contrast, in the book of Hebrews chapter 3, the Word talks about Israel who saw God's works for forty years, yet still did not know His ways. This led them to perish and remains a powerful warning. It illustrates that a focus on works does not bring an intimate relationship or knowledge of God. The right way to access our authority to minister healing and wholeness to others is by coming through Jesus into His kingdom family first.

I did not name this book. It named itself. It is an expression that automatically flows out of my mouth every time I see God's handiwork, His impeccable timing, and how He seamlessly coordinates multiple events that have impossible odds of happening. What some would call coincidence, I call Holy Ghost. Embedded in these impossible odds, we see God revealing a key portion of His personality and nature. Begin to pay close attention, not only to what He does but how He does it. No detail is random or wasted in the hands of our Creator.

Allow me to share a bit about my upbringing to give you a glimpse into why these truths have become so precious in my daily life. I grew up in a traditional denominational household. I went to Religious Grammar School. I served as an altar boy. Religion was a part of the environment that shaped my early childhood. Typical school days included prayer and religious study. On special Holy Days, we walked over to the church for services. We memorized much about the life of Jesus along with other important historical biblical figures such as Moses, Noah, and King David. I was learning part of what it means to be a Christian. There was only one problem. Despite the fact that we learned about God, we didn't get to know Him. Knowledge is not equal to relationship. Access to God's heart comes by way of real relationship.

Have you ever followed a celebrity, a sports figure, or a high-tech entrepreneur as a fan? If so, you are aware that it is possible to study many aspects of a life or a career. You may know their biography, education, and accomplishments. But at the end of the day, you still do not know the person. Studying them from a distance only reveals their public persona, a reality which is often vastly different from the real individual. Our modern day fascination with social media is creating an even higher level of this illusion of relationship. To get to know a person, you have to get up close and personal. Simply stated, you must do real life together. That is the only way. Shadowing, observing, and following only give us a partial, impersonal glimpse into the life of online friends and admired celebrities.

It is much the same with Jesus. Studying His life and ministry from a distance will never equate to a desire to know Him as a friend, brother, or father.

Knowing Jesus in an intimate way requires more than shadowing Him in daily life. It requires a deep desire to know and to be known. While shadowing implies being near a person to observe them, God is waiting for an invitation to fill and overtake us while also allowing us to hide in Him. Do you want Jesus and His Holy Spirit to know you intimately while allowing you to get to know Him? I sure do! That passion is at the heart of why I have chosen to write this book.

Look at the review of the church in Revelation chapter 2. They were commended for many things only to be rebuked for abandoning their first love. This Scripture is a timeless reminder of what we are often missing in our lives today: an intimate, real relationship.

Distant observation will never lead to a life of intimacy with our Creator. That requires moving beyond mere religion as we walk through the door of life into real relationship. Remember, Jesus is the only door. Works and performance are counterfeits made to look appealing by the enemy in an attempt to get us to miss God altogether.

While some people miss God while trying hard to serve Him through tasks and action, there is another reason which I relate to. I was led to believe early on that a relationship with God was reserved for those far more important or special than I would ever be. I grew up in a man made religious system that determined who was holy and sinless, thereby determining those who met the requirements needed to know God. There is a big problem with this type of system. My childhood experience was not grounded in truth. Man cannot earn the right to know God intimately by jumping through religious hoops. It takes a life of surrender and love to begin knowing Him. We get to know God in ways similar to our closest family and friends. Relationship deepens as we spend time together, especially when the desire exists to love and to be loved.

Jesus is a friend of sinners. That is the beauty of who He is. It took me a long time to discover that. When I did, my life was changed forever. I was a sinner when I met Him, but the moment I invited Jesus into my heart, I took my place as a son of God. For that reason, this book is not about the evangelists that speak to crowds of thousands or those who have a television show or write best sellers. It's about the common person, the ordinary person.

I don't want this book to be about me either. Instead, I want stories from my life to illustrate that your stories also matter, and that God is waiting to minister to you and through you. This book is a glimpse into a perfect God choosing to partner with imperfect people to bring about healing and wholeness to those locked in darkness. My story is a micro picture of His story as Jesus has invited each son and daughter to represent Him right where they live, work, play, and grow.

While some of these stories are tremendously powerful by nature, many of them are about seemingly small things. God is concerned with everything pertaining to you and your life. He is in all the details, great and small. If something is important to you, it's important to Him. Whether you are facing an incurable disease or have simply lost your car keys, Jesus is with you one hundred percent.

That's the God I love and serve. To honor the God I have come to know through an intimate relationship, I have chosen to compile the stories you now hold in your hand. These testimonies accumulated through a lifetime of relationship with Jesus Christ. Despite my flaws and failures along the way, He has never left me.

This book is nothing more than an example of the kind of relationship that you can have with Him. I am not suggesting that you should try to copy my actions. Instead, I am challenging you to allow my experiences to ignite a fire within that leaves you longing to steward every dream He holds for you.

This book exists to honor Jesus and remind you of the life that awaits the passionate lover of Christ. First and foremost, Jesus loves you. Never forget that. The Bible promises that He will never leave or forsake His children, whether in good times or in bad.

Jesus longs to know you and He wants to do the miraculous through you. Resist the enemy and come with me as we press into God, the place where every ordinary person becomes truly extraordinary.

Take a moment to evaluate your own heart and belief system. It is crucial that we align our hearts according to the complete truth of the Word of God, especially when His truth is counter to the world around us. If we are not careful, we will fall into the trap of deception, and this can cause us to miss our true identity and destiny. Don't allow yourself to say, "I am not worthy." Don't say, "I don't know enough about the Bible." Don't say, "Signs, wonders, and miracles are a thing of the past."

God is always willing to show His glory through ordinary people.

Jesus said John 14:12, "whoever believes in me will also do the works that I do; and greater works."

If you belong to Jesus by faith, then "the Spirit of

him that raised up Jesus from the dead dwell in you, he that raised up Christ from the dead shall also quicken your mortal bodies by his Spirit that dwelleth in you." Romans 8:11 (KJV) The Holy Spirit lives in you. Take another moment and allow that to really sink in.

Where you are on your journey is not what matters most. Whether you are a new Believer or a seasoned follower of Jesus, this book exists to make you hungry for more of God. What matters is that there is always another level to discover when following God. My heart is that we refuse to grow complacent, bored, or disillusioned with the Kingdom of God, and especially with the King of kings Himself.

I especially want to encourage those who are new to this life of faith. You may not have many of your own stories yet (or perhaps you have not learned how to identify and value the ones that already exist), but I am here to encourage you to develop that relationship with Him. Fruit comes as a relationship develops over time, just as fruit grows on a healthy, maturing tree in due time. In much the same way as the early disciples, we were created by God to know Him and to partner with Him as He brings light into a dark world.

He said, "I will not leave you as orphans; I will come to you." John 14:18

That is why He sent the Holy Spirit. If you have placed your faith in Jesus as Savior, then you are no longer an orphan, but a true son or daughter. That is the Good News! It is imperative that each person press in to learn all that He holds in store for His Kingdom family.

The living God who created us to know Him and to partner with Him deserves our best. Put Jesus first in everything you do. This single decision aligns you with the heart of the One who loved you before time began. As we focus on Him and His will for us, the stories flow as He continues to reach the world through our lives. Allow His light to shine in your heart. Every step you take with Him will cause your own collection of stories to emerge. Even if you don't envision writing a book, I encourage you to journal. This provides a personal archive of God's faithfulness in your life that will empower you when you struggle and fuel your passion when you are strong. Perhaps your own journal will be used to challenge the generations to come.

You can't make this up—but Jesus can!

Chapter 1
AN INVITATION TO COME HOME

For still the vision awaits its appointed time;
it hastens to the end—it will not lie. If it seems slow,
wait for it; it will surely come; it will not delay.

HABAKKUK 2:3

For years, the thought of writing this book weighed on my heart. Two years ago, this compelling idea was confirmed by a dear brother in the Lord as he spoke into my life. Now is the time for this personal collection of testimonies to be released for God's glory.

Even as I was getting started on writing this book, I had yet another incredible you can't make this up—but Jesus can experience. The Lord used this divine moment as His endorsement on the timing of this project as it began to move out of the vision phase and onto paper.

I met a young man two years ago named Christian and he has humbly given me permission to share parts of his story. With a name like that, you know God has great plans for this young man. Later, there will be a section dedicated to Christian and how I have been impacted by his journey over the last two years. But for now, I'm just going to share this particular divine moment. Christian is a young man with a broken early life who I befriended at the leading of the Lord. At the time of this writing, he is 18 years old.

Today, as I was writing, his name appeared in the newspaper. Unfortunately, he made the local news due to having been arrested for multiple felonies. His bail was set at $335,000. Facing years of incarceration, Christian desperately needs the Lord to intervene on his behalf and I choose to believe that the Lord will show him mercy.

Despite his obvious mistakes, Christian has an incredible heart like few people I have ever met. His recent arrests and behavior simply do not reflect what God showed me to be true of his heart. He has been influenced to do certain things that go against the core of who he really is. While that does not excuse his mistakes, it is a powerful lesson on how easy it is to follow the ways of the world instead of walking in our God-given identity in Christ. What happens in our young years has such a huge impact on our perspective of the world around us.

Last winter I gave him a new, heavy winter coat. A few days later as we were driving downtown, I stopped at a red light. We both took note of a homeless man on the corner. While I sat with my foot on the brake, Christian spontaneously jumped out of the car, took off his new coat, and handed it to the homeless man. In that moment, I saw Christian tapping into the man he truly is. I believe God took note of his actions which were born out of pure compassion. While God does not overlook sinful behavior (even good earthly fathers discipline their children), I will always be convinced that God looks at our hearts and knows our intentions with the wisdom and pride of a father.

The devil sets traps for young people every day. Perhaps he knows the love and redemption that would be unleashed to our communities if every young person began walking in true destiny. Sure, he sets traps for people of all ages, but here is why I make this age distinction. Satan desires to derail destinies early in our lives, He knows how hard it can be to get back on track once you have been labeled by society and even by yourself as a loser.

Despite all my efforts to help Christian move toward a relationship with Jesus, I currently feel like a complete failure as his friend and mentor. I am trying to remind myself that all the seeds planted will one day bear fruit, while the facts of the present day are screaming the opposite. This inner conflict leaves me with painful and difficult questions to answer. Was there something more I could have done? Should I have said something different? What did I miss along the way? How could I have helped him make better life choices?

The news headlines today highlighting his mistakes left my mind is swirling with questions! My heart is truly broken.

I decided to look for an intentional way to get my mind off this news today. That decision led me to take a deep dive into finally moving this book project forward. It was high time to stop wading around in the shallow waters of thinking about it and finally just do it! I thought it would be a good way to keep my mind focused on the goodness of God. I needed personally reminded of how my Heavenly Father keeps His promises.

I am keeping a favorite verse in focus both for this young man and myself. Let's look at this amazing promise in a couple of different translations. While Christian desperately needs to take hold of this verse, I am humbled and reminded that we each will find our own identity and purpose strengthened when we link our choices to this great promise.

"For I know the plans I have for you, declares the Lord, plans for welfare and not for evil, to give you a future and a hope." Jeremiah 29:11

"I'll show up and take care of you as I promised and bring you back home. I know what I am doing. I have it all planned out—plans to take care of you, not to abandon you, plans to give you the future you hope for." Jeremiah 29:11 (The Message)

This passage was written to Israel just before they went into captivity. It was meant as an anchor of hope to carry them through the difficult years ahead.

My decision to write today was quickly followed by a need to find the perfect location to exercise my typing fingers and my creativity. Where an athlete needs a gym, a writer needs a great coffee shop. I chose my local Barnes and Noble bookstore. All the tables are two-seaters except the back area which features two large round tables that can each accommodate five people. I like being able to spread out, keeping my drink at a safe distance from my laptop, while also enjoying that sense of a creative space. I arrived and got set for a serious session of writing with God. My large table was quickly filled. Hot chai, a blueberry muffin, a heart overflowing with testimonies, and I was ready to go.

After just a few minutes, three young people sat down at the table next to me. I later learned their names were Steven, Candice, and Daniel. The tables are positioned close together so I couldn't help overhearing keywords like Christ, Jesus, Christian, Church, and so on. I sensed Holy Spirit might just be up to something, so I tuned in to His voice. It was becoming clear that the Lord had directed me to this place—right down to this specific table—for His purpose.

When disappointments come, the devil is right there with one of his favorite demonic henchmen. His familiar name is Depression. If you have lived long enough, you may have done battle with him yourself. Depression is a real disembodied spirit. I recognize him all too well. Every person alive needs to know how to put this demonic oppressor on the run the same way an alarm forces a burglar away from a residence. "Be gone in Jesus' name," should always be our response whenever we feel him trespassing.

While the medical and scientific world would refer to depression as a condition or a mental illness, make no mistake about it. This mental tormentor is often at the epicenter of attack against any human mind and heart. Please understand here that I am not minimizing or making light of the millions of people who struggle with depression. I am sharing my own experience that has proven to me that successfully waging war includes spiritual warfare.

David was also familiar with this spirit. He saw it working actively in the life of Saul and he even did battle with this demonic force himself. The name Philistine means "to wallow in self-pity like a pig in the mud." Self-pity often partners with depression in an attack designed to distract and derail an individual's focus. When I think of my own experiences battling this enemy, those moments were typically linked with feeling sorry for myself and doubting myself.

David battled and won many times against the Philistines, in part, symbolizing his determination to overcome depression and self-pity. By doing so, he shared a timeless strategy that still works today.

I have learned that the most practical solution is to keep moving forward. That is what I chose to do as I ventured to find my perfect writer's spot today. The newspaper headline about my friend could have caused sabotaged my day. It would have been easy to stay on the couch while wallowing in worry, fear, and anxiety. Instead, I chose to write from a place of faith and perspective in an effort to put this demonic spirit of depression to flight. In short, I had to evict this spirit out of my day and my assignment. I strongly encourage you to do the same.

I was always taught that it is rude to eavesdrop on a private conversation, but I forgot my etiquette as this group of young adults captured my attention. Their backs were to me except for Steven. I was a bit bummed because this made it harder to grasp all they were saying. While I try not to be rude, I felt the Lord lingering in their conversation and my heart really needed recalibrating. So, I hung on the words I could catch. This was no ordinary conversation. I was drawn in by their conviction and their joy.

Our culture typically expects young people to talk about school, dating, fashion, and other self-focused and empty topics. We don't give our youth the respect they often deserve. Perhaps this is why some like Christian find it hard to obtain a higher mark, as society has set the bar low on the upcoming generations. This conversation was blowing my mind. Here was a group of young adults choosing to talk about Jesus and I wanted to know it all. Etiquette flew out the window as I leaned in their direction.

Keywords I overheard included artwork and Christian artists. After some time passed, they decided to adjourn for a dinner break, so I seized the opportunity to speak to them. "Excuse me, I couldn't help but over-hear your conversation. Is one of you a Christian art-ist?" Candice replied "no" and asks why I was curious. I explained that I am a local pastor and I am always interested in that sort of thing.

At that moment, the flood gates of conversation opened. Mutual connections and connectedness in the Spirit began to flow freely. We knew many of the same people. Steven's pastor is a friend of mine. Candice is deeply interested in divine healing and I had just returned from a three-day healing seminar in Texas. I gave her the name of the main teacher there so she could check out his ministry. They were new Christians who shared a deep hunger for more of God, so I began to pour into them as much as I could on a variety of subjects.

I hadn't seen this much hunger in a long time. As we connected, my heart was being renewed, as Je-sus reminded me that He is going with me just as that verse in Jeremiah promises.

Jesus said to His disciples after ministering to the woman at the well, "I have food to eat that you do not know about." John 4:32 He was expressing how satis-fying life can be when we obey Him in ministry. Obe-dience to God brings maturity and becomes food for your soul.

I have been on many mission trips where the crowd that gathered had a tangible spiritual hunger for God. In these settings, it feels as if every word spoken and ministered is like seed that quickly germinates into fruit in the lives of those willing to enter into His presence. Jesus comes on the scene the moment He senses our hunger. It is true just as Scripture promises that those who look for God will find Him. He is faithful to pour Himself out on the hungry and the thirsty. "Blessed are those who hunger and thirst for righteousness, for they shall be satisfied." Matthew 5:6

Just a few moments of conversation united us as friends. I could feel hope rise again in my own heart. Overwhelmed, I turned to them and told them how re-freshing it was to hear their hearts come alive for Jesus. Then Candice looked me straight in the eye and deliv-ered the silver bullet. She said to me, "and there are a lot of us out there!" Oh God, where are they? I want to pour into them with everything I have and everything I am. That simple truth is at the core of why I have cho-sen to write this book, for people like the ones I just met! It is also why I refuse to give up on Christian. God is drawing each person to Himself, and His heart will not rest until all His sons and daughters come home.

You can't make this up—but Jesus can!

Chapter 2
FIRST MIRACLES

The lampstand also for the light ... and the oil for the light.

Exodus 35:14

One of the first miracles I experienced (other than the gifts of salvation and Holy Spirit baptism) is one I will always remember. I was in my mid-twenties and a new Christian. My wife and I already had two sons and a home on Long Island in New York. Our home was small at just under five hundred square feet. It could be said that we were ahead of our time, as the tiny house movement booms today.

Our bedroom could not even hold a traditional bedroom set—only the bed and a dresser. Even our nightstands had no place in this minimalistic space. This little old tiny house was especially drafty in the winter due to being poorly insulated. Termites had eaten the wood under the kitchen sink on the outside wall. So, in the winter, your toes went numb when washing the dishes. In the summer, your toes enjoyed the island breeze while standing in the same spot at the kitchen sink.

This home was heated with oil, so despite being so small, it was expensive to keep warm in the harsh winter season. There were many times when we could only afford to buy five gallons of fuel at a time, and that only gained my growing family another day or two of warmth.

Many of those older homes had standard size, 275-gallon tanks in their basements to store fuel. A handy gauge on top of the tank allowed the family adults to monitor the remaining fuel so they would not run out of heat. It was unsafe for children to be around.

Looking back, our oil tank seemed even older than the little house. The gauge had gone missing, so convenience was lost. I had to climb up, unscrew the cap, and lower a stick into the huge tank, much like a person would check the oil in a car engine. I kept close tabs on the fragile inches of fuel remaining in an effort to avoid running out of fuel over a cold night. I was broke but diligent. Looking back, it was a stress on my heart in that season as I longed to provide well for my deserving family.

One particularly cold night, I measured the tank and found that we were down to just an inch or two. I knew it was barely enough to keep us warm through the night. I would lay in bed at night and listen for the oil burner to kick on. In my mind's eye, I would see a picture of a gas pump with the meter spinning and the dollars running out of control. Fear and anxiety were never far away.

It is not advisable to let these tanks go all the way empty. They pick up rust and sediment that lies near the bottom of the tank and this can clog up the filter and oil burner. With two babies in the house, it was not an ideal situation. I don't remember my exact prayer. I just know that I decided to pray. At this point, I did not have much history with God, but that did not stop Him from showing up.

God was about to show me a new facet of who He is: Jehovah Jireh. I learned in that season that the best prayer for a young Christian is simply, "HELP!" Think back to your childhood. You probably don't have to recall too many memories before you run into one or more in which you asked your mom, dad, or grandparent for help. God is our perfect Father. He is always on call, ready, and willing to help.

The next day, for whatever reason, I decided to

check our fuel level again. Sometimes when you receive a personal miracle or distinct answer to prayer, you are stunned and find yourself rehearsing what just took place. To my amazement, there were twenty-five inches of oil in the tank. I was shocked. I felt as if I had just won the lottery even though the financial value was not worth millions. I remember thinking to myself, "God really cares for me and my family. He is concerned for me. I am not alone!"

That sounds so basic to a seasoned Christian, but I was not a seasoned Christian by any means. I was more like a young child in the process of discovering I had a Father who loved me. To a hungry man, a simple slice of bread can taste like a gourmet meal. Those few inches of fuel ignited my faith just as much as if God had filled my tank completely full.

This was just the start of an amazing journey that I would come to recognize as my own miracle-filled life. Let me remind you of a crucial truth. I am not more special than you or anyone else. You and I are sons and daughters of God, equally valued as His own creation. This is the heart of the Father toward every human being who chooses to hunger after His presence and provision. Lord, please help me to remember that you never fail to care for even the smallest details of my life!

What do you need to trust Him for? What spiritual, or natural, resources are you running low on? Perhaps you need peace, wisdom, direction, heat for your home, or a tank of gas for your car. Ask! He loves to answer and provide for His own.

You can't make this up—but Jesus can!

Chapter 3
SAVED BY A CHRISTMAS GIFT

But the Lord is faithful. He will establish you
and guard you against the evil one.

2 THESSALONIANS 3:3

I am truly ok with the fact that our first home was small, old, and drafty. Great things often have humble beginnings. Despite being size challenged, I remember that place as if it was a palace. Why? For at least one powerful reason. This is also the home where I was baptized in the Holy Spirit. Yes, you heard me right. I was not in church. I was at home when the power of God descended on my life in a new and glorious way. You might say it was the beginning of my personal Pentecost.

Prior to that life-altering event, there were several unusual happenings.

For starters, my brother sometimes gave unusual gifts. For our first Christmas in the house, he gave us a fire extinguisher. I remained gracious and thankful. Then I placed the odd gift in the basement, near my oil tank just to get it out of our way. The following January, I was in the basement doing laundry soon after my second son Michael was born.

The washer and dryer were situated next to the oil-burning furnace. As I moved clothes from the washer to the dryer, the burner cycled on. There was nothing unusual about that. Remember, that was my cue that my family was warm, at least for the near future. But then, something out of the ordinary caught my eye. Flames came shooting out of the top. Then, the entire oil burner went up in flames. It continued running as the pump kept pushing fuel oil into the system.

The entire house was about to go up in flames!

Randomly situated right next to me was the fire extinguisher, barely one-month-old. I simply pulled the pin, aimed as instructed, and squeezed the handle. Situation handled! My brother's quirky gift became the solution to what could have been a devastating tragedy. While I credit him for his gift, I also credit God for directing my placement of the gift and the timing of my laundry duty. My new fire extinguisher saved my young family's life. This moment still serves as a reminder that God is my protector and His direction and timing are perfect. It is my job to tune in to His voice and prompting continually in my daily life.

There was another situation in this home which added to a somewhat odd beginning. The house had previously been occupied by an elderly couple. One day, according to the neighbors, the husband disappeared and was never seen again. Years later after his wife passed away, their daughter sold the house to us.

While working in the garage, I had discovered some strange artifacts. There were books with odd passages underlined, bank books, documents of UFO sightings, and all manner of weird objects. The most disturbing was a voodoo doll of a woman with strings tightly wound around one arm and needles stuck in an eye. My wife and I discussed it with a neighbor only to find out that the woman who lived there was paralyzed in one arm and blind in one eye. We promptly burned all the artifacts.

Brothers and Sister in the Lord, such things are not toys nor are they to be played with. Scripture says, "Your adversary the devil prowls around like a roaring lion, seeking someone to devour." 1 Peter 5:8

Now if you are in Christ, you have nothing to fear. A true Believer is only called to a holy, reverential fear of God, not man or the devil. Scripture also says, "Behold, I have given you authority to tread on serpents and scorpions, and over all the power of the enemy, and nothing shall hurt you." Luke 10:19

We need to learn to recognize his evil schemes, put on our protective shield of prayer, and cast down every vain imagination. As we read in 2 Corinthians 10:5, "We destroy arguments and every lofty opinion raised against the knowledge of God and take every thought captive to obey Christ." We should never tempt God by making the things of Satan food for our own curiosity. The true Christian has no business playing with the occult. Things like ouija boards, tarot cards, fortune tellers, ghost hunters, and past times designed to honor or summon other gods are not to be trifled with. Do not give place to these things. Certainly, there is danger involved. Most importantly, God deserves to be honored as the one true Father, King of kings, and Lord of lords.

You can't make this up—but Jesus can!

Chapter 4
BEE ALIVE

How sweet are your words to my taste,
sweeter than honey to my mouth!

PSALM 119:103

This story is about my second son Michael. He has a tender and compassionate heart. Like any parent, it grieves you to see your child suffer in any way. Michael suffered from asthma as a young child. His case was severe, affecting his breathing capacity several times a year. When the seasons changed, the asthma would become a brutal, life-threatening battle. His breathing would become labored and his chest would begin to swell. Many times, this required frightening trips to the emergency room for immediate treatment.

I was a young father and a young Christian at the time. Out of desperation and obedience, I franticly sought God and prayed for Michael's healing. I believed wholeheartedly that God was a Healer, but I still wasn't quite sure how it all worked. Whether or not God would show up in response to my prayers seemed somewhat random. That didn't make sense and I wasn't sure if it was God's will to heal all the time.

Even though I was a young Christian I had already witnessed several miracles. I had the faith to believe that God would heal but I didn't know the approach. This began a long search for the truth about divine healing which I will cover later in this book.

In the early days, when I would pray, I expected God to move in some dramatic way. I had growing faith and could easily believe for a special visitation or some powerful demonstration of God. As I began to pray over this troubling health situation with my own son, I sensed an unusual and unexpected leading of the Lord for the solution. I heard about a nutritional supplement called Royal Jelly, a substance produced in the beehive which provides special food exclusively for the queen bee. This substance which is high in amino acids has been proven to strengthen the body's immune system. At first, I was disappointed that God would choose to use this method for Michael's healing. I was looking for something more miraculous and more immediate.

It seemed that the Lord was going to teach me another dimension of faith and healing, thereby revealing another aspect of His nature. As I continued studying and praying, I was led to read the story about Naaman the leper. He was looking for healing too. If you remember the story, Naaman was told to go wash seven times in the Jordan River and when he heard this suggestion, he was offended.

Much like me at this time, he expected Elijah to call upon the name of the Lord to release some dramatic experience for his healing. "But Naaman was angry and went away, saying, 'Behold, I thought that he would surely come out to me and stand and call upon the name of the Lord his God, and wave his hand over the place and cure the leper.'" 2 Kings 5:11 At first, he went away filled with pride and anger. Finally, out of desperation, he submitted to the instructions of Elijah and dipped seven times in the Jordan. When he obeyed the unique request, he was healed. His skin was completely restored.

As I considered what God had placed on my heart and after reading that story, I placed an order for Royal Jelly. Part of my frustration, knowing that God could heal my son instantly, emerged when I realized it was going to cost over seventy dollars for a one-month supply. Back then, that amount of money felt like seven hundred dollars. I sighed and placed the order.

When your children are sick, you spare no expense.

The Royal Jelly came in a form similar in texture to honey or peanut butter. We fed it to Michael faithfully for one month. This required getting creative. We would spread it on toast in the morning as part of his breakfast.

When the month's supply was exhausted, he was healed. That marked the last asthma attack he ever had. Seventy dollars and one month later, my son was finally free from this brutal attacker.

Michael is now in his late-30s and has been healthy ever since. Not only was he cured of asthma, but we learned much through the experience. While I believe in the natural properties found in Royal Jelly, I honestly believe that our family's obedience to the Word of the Lord was the key that God used to unlock this magnificent healing.

While God is able to heal and move apart from my partnership, one of the greatest miracles of all is that He wants me—and you—to become part of His intervention.

Since He lives in me, I invite Jesus daily to work through me. Our obedience and submission matters, as it can impact the lives of those we love and serve.

You can't make this up—but Jesus can!

Chapter 5
MOVED BY COMPASSION

My daughter has just died, but come and
lay your hand on her, and she will live.

MATTHEW 9:18

I have four children. They are uniquely awesome and will never know how much they mean to me.

When it comes to the miraculous process of childbirth, my wife deserved the award for bravery. Using only breathing techniques and God's help, she brought all four of our children into this world with no painkillers, medications or epidural. To be there as the father and witness all four births was an unrivaled experience in my life. Few memories even come close to how precious these moments were. To witness a human birth is truly one of life's great miracles. The blessing of becoming a mother or a father is God's gift to us.

The fourth and final birth, my youngest daughter

Keri, was the most difficult. Despite the doctor's best efforts, the placenta did not fully release. Rather than continue with what was already a dangerous and painful process, the doctor released her to go home with the intention of performing a D & C some days later.

I remember sitting on the couch in our den. My wife was curled up in a ball, with a heating pad pressed into her stomach, unable to move because of the severe pain. As if the pain of childbirth wasn't enough, going back to the doctor was the last thing in the world she wanted to do. She had just gotten released from the hospital. The thought of returning seemed far too taxing and overwhelming.

There was almost nothing I could do for her. My mind drifted to the fact that my maternal grandmother had died tragically two weeks after my mother's birth from basically the same condition that my wife was now facing. I could have easily felt helpless, but I was learning where to turn in times of trouble. As I flipped through the pages of my Bible, I came across the story of the woman with the issue of blood. You may be familiar with the story. If not, it is found in Luke 8:43. I encourage you to take time to read it for yourself. In that culture, she was considered unclean and was to refrain from contact with other people. She had been in this condition for a long time and she had spent all her money on doctors without relief. She was left isolated and desperate. Her story is a powerful reminder of how Satan tries to isolate you from those who can help in times of trouble.

Much like the woman in this story, my wife and I were desperate. The strange thing is I did not pray for my wife. This time, there was no laying on of hands and no prayer circle. I simply whispered to the Lord, "If you could heal this woman in the Bible, then you could do this for my wife." I leaned hard into my faith as I reminded God of what I knew He could do.

Miraculously and to our great delight, she was healed by our Great Physician. It was almost as if we were reliving that great record of healing from Luke 8. Even today, I am reminded of the way Scripture captured that moment as it was also recorded in the book of Mark: "she could feel in her body that she had been healed of her terrible condition" Mark 5:29 (NLT).

When Jesus was moved with compassion, miracles happened. Today, as Jesus is moved by our compassion, miracles still happen.

You can't make this up—but Jesus can!

Chapter 6

SOMETIMES THE WORLD
COMES TO YOU

Go into all the world and proclaim
the gospel to the whole creation.

MARK 16:15

My early days walking with God were a complex mix of zeal and frustration. I was on fire for God and I wanted to go. I just didn't know where. I felt compelled to do something. Something I could not quite define was burning in me.

The stark reality was that I had a family, a job, and a home to care for. Staying put seemed the responsible thing to do. In retrospect, I regret now that I did not trust the Lord enough to just take my family and dive head-first into a life of ministry. That was my heart. In fact, that is what God told me to do. Instead, I let people talk me into being sensible, logical, and "wise."

When another Christian tells you to use wisdom, exercise caution. Many times, it is sugar-coated fear trying to latch on to you. In the passage recorded in Mark 14:3, the woman pours expensive ointment upon Jesus's head. She is ridiculed by onlookers because they said it could have been sold and the money given to the poor. They were basically saying she did not use wisdom. Jesus commended her and rightfully so.

In my situation, well-meaning fellow Believers who told me to use wisdom had fallen prey to believing that a life of typical work and drudgery somehow proved a man's loyalty to his family. I know their intentions were good, but they forgot one key truth. As a son of God, I am called to follow His voice and not the voice of man. While God may call an individual to work in a traditional way to feed his family, God had called me toward a different path.

My mistake was placing more weight on the voices of men than the voice of God. Because God was dealing with me in a personal manner, what some called wisdom turned into a trap set by the enemy. I still bear the burden of those regrets. The only recorded time Jesus said "wait" was when He told the disciples to wait in Jerusalem for the power of the Holy Ghost. "And while staying with them he ordered them not to depart from Jerusalem, but to wait for the promise of the Father, which, he said, "you heard from me." Acts 1:4

In the Old Testament, Joshua and Caleb were ready to follow God's leading to a new place. They were not afraid of reports of the giants living in what they knew to be their new promised land. Sometimes fear or a lack of faith can cause our enemy to appear larger than he actually is! Because of fear that gripped the hearts of the other spies, the majority won out. This meant that Joshua and Caleb had to surrender their vision and bravery to the collective choice to play small in the face of fear, a devastating mistake that led the Israelites to endure wandering in the desert, despite a new life being clearly in view.

I can relate to how those brave men must have felt when they found no one else they could share this new land and new life with. Like the Israelites, I was trapped without a significant way out. I was holding fast to the promised land of the Gospel message I had so recently discovered, and yet, I had nowhere to carry this message.

Although Joshua was delayed, he was not dismayed. God put his time in the desert to good use and eventually honored his faith.

I can honestly say now as I look back that I can relate to the frustration that the bold few must have felt. I remember one day when this frustration reached a high point as I was making a delivery for work up to

Newburgh, New York. Once every week I made this trip which was about a three-hour drive each way. The truck had just an AM radio, a fun fact that is hard to imagine with today's new auto technology. If you had a cassette player in your car back in those days, you were riding high.

Since I only had that old radio, I also kept a portable cassette player on the seat so I could listen to Amy Grant or Keith Green as I drove. These were the new generation of musicians who shared my heart for the Gospel message at the time. Keith Green's lyrics had a way of stoking the fire in my bones. I had learned that private worship time was a favorite way of connecting to the heart of God.

In those days I had a habit of giving rides to hitch-hikers to lighten their burden and gain an opportunity to share Jesus with them. On this particular day, I saw a man alongside the New York State Thruway. People did not normally beg rides along this route since it is illegal, so I pulled the truck over to the side and popped the door open.

This man was energetic and young, perhaps in his early twenties. For some reason, I could not quite pinpoint his nationality. A quick assessment led me to believe that he was not American.

I asked where he was headed, and it turned out that he was on his way to a funeral. When I asked where he was from, I was jolted in my seat. He answered simply, "Israel." There is a town in upstate New York called Rome, but definitely no Israel. I could not believe what I was hearing. I had just picked up a man from the country of Israel on the side of the New York State Thruway.

He explained that his journey to America was for the funeral of a friend. I could only surmise that it must be for someone extremely important in his life since he had chosen to travel halfway around the world.

I jumped at this opportunity to share Jesus. We had a great conversation and the seeds of the Gospel were planted in his heart. After I dropped him off, I marveled at the ways of God.

When Jesus was twelve years old, He taught in the temple and stayed behind when His parents left Jerusalem. When questioned by His parents He said He was about His Father's business. It also says that He subjected Himself to His parents after that. "And he went down with them and came to Nazareth and was submissive to them. And his mother treasured up all these things in her heart." Luke 2:51

The Apostle Paul wrote most of the New Testament while sitting in a jail cell. Even imprisonment could not keep the Gospel message from going forth.

My zealous frustration calmed down after that day as I realized that Holy Spirit is with me wherever I go. Physical limitations do not stop the Spirit of God.

I have often wondered what God did in his life as a result of this encounter and upon his return to his home country.

You can't make this up—but Jesus can!

Chapter 7
THE OVERNIGHT HEALING

He rose and immediately picked up his bed and went
out before them all, so that they were all amazed and
glorified God, saying, "We never saw anything like this!"

MARK 2:12

Sometimes divine healing is immediate and sometimes it is progressive. I like to think of it in terms of instant miracles and the reversal of a disease or infirmity
that requires recovery time for the body to be made
whole again.

In the writings of John G. Lake from the turn of the
century, this legendary minister records both instant
healings as well as healings that were progressive and
took time to manifest. I have concluded that the enemy
resists God any way he can; therefore, we should walk
by faith and refuse to stop praying until the job is done.

At one point in my work life, I had my own business
in construction and roofing. During this period, I had

no personal health insurance. My knowledge of healing was still quite limited despite having seen many things that God could do.

Out of nowhere, I developed a ganglion cyst on the top of my foot. It grew and grew until it looked like someone had cut a golf ball in half and inserted it under my skin. It was becoming difficult to get my shoes on as well as to tolerate the pressure this caused. I could not afford to stop working and I had no way to pay for a medical consultation.

This story brings a powerful reminder. Desperation is a great prayer motivator. I had nowhere to turn except to God. I brought my need straight to the Lord. Not yet fully aware of the authority we each have as Believers over sickness and disease, He lovingly blessed me in my innocence and desperation.

At the time, I was part of a charismatic Episcopal Church. They were well-meaning and kind. There was a priest who would come through on occasion who was said to have a healing ministry. At that time, the claims about the healing minister reinforced my wrong belief that certain people had a healing gift and you had to seek them out to get your healing.

This priest was scheduled to come on a certain day,

and I was not going to miss my touch from Heaven. I needed healing!

The night before his service, I went to bed as usual. I remember being excited in faith that I would be prayed for the next day. I fully believed I would come away from that gathering whole and healed with a shoe that fit well on a normal foot.

There was just one problem. If you go expecting healing, you need to have something wrong with you.

When I woke up the next morning the cyst was completely gone! Vanished! Not a trace! I was over the top excited and amazed. Even though I had been looking forward to seeing it happen in church, I was beside myself. I still went to the service because I knew it would be a great experience. There I witnessed a young woman who was deaf in both ears receive her miracle of having her hearing restored.

God was teaching me two key lessons.

While God clearly anoints men and women of faith, the opportunity to minister healing is not reserved for a special few. This is a blessing made available to every follower of Jesus Christ. Jesus can heal through anyone's true faith.

The Lord was also showing me, as He did many times in those early days, not to depend on any man. You do not have to wait for the faith healer to travel through your town when you are in need or you know someone in need. God is with you now.

These early lessons have stayed with me all these years!

If you have always longed for the authority to minister divine healing to those in need, begin to step out in faith. Your faith and obedience to Jesus gives you the authority to pray for the sick according to His Word. Believers will lay hands on the sick and they will recover. "They will pick up serpents with their hands; and if they drink any deadly poison, it will not hurt them; they will lay their hands on the sick, and they will recover." Mark 16:18

Years later, while living in Florida, my youngest daughter Keri developed a similar cyst on the inside of her wrist the size of a marble. The negative reports flowed: she will need surgery, there is the danger of cutting a nerve, you need to use wisdom, be realistic. I knew what God had done for me and I chose to believe that same healing power was available for my daughter.

We anointed her with oil and prayed in a Sunday service. Nothing happened, so we repeated that process by faith the next Sunday. Within a day or two it was completely gone and never returned. This healing also reinforced the power we have as a faith community when we gather and join our faith to pray for the needs in our midst. I was grateful for my faith and the faith of our church community.

Herein lies another powerful reminder. Stand on the report of previous victories to encourage yourself (and those in need) for the mountain you are facing today. Testimonies of healing prime the atmosphere, thereby building our faith and expectation. In 1 Samuel 30:6 when David found himself in trouble, we are told that he strengthened himself in the Lord.

You can't make this up—but Jesus can!

Chapter 8
THE ULTIMATE COME BACK

For still the vision awaits its appointed time;
it hastens to the end—it will not lie. If it seems slow,
wait for it; it will surely come; it will not delay.

HABAKKUK 2:3

In the fall of 1985, I had a dream. Since the beginning of my relationship with God, Holy Spirit has communicated many things to me through dreams. Sometimes the dreams are metaphors representing events and other times they are literal, detailed, and exact. This dream was a combination of both. The dream was short and to the point. I was standing on the roof of the business where I worked. A huge storm came with high winds and as I stood on the roof, I was not moved by the storm. But the roof was ripped off around me like you would peel an orange.

The business where I worked at that time had started in the owner's basement. When I began working there it was located in a small, rented building. I was employed by this business when I was first saved and baptized in the Holy Ghost. The owner was a religious man, but he seemed at times to be afraid of what he did not understand. I share this not out of judgment, but to set the stage for what was yet to come in the story.

At one point, he told me not to read my Bible in the building during my lunch break. I honored his request and found an easy solution. I just went outside and read in the company truck while I listened to speakers like Chuck Smith and R.W. Schambach on the AM radio.

It was readily evident that God was blessing this business.

Fast forward a few years. The company experienced explosive growth. We had just moved into a custom built 17,500 square foot building which housed manufacturing, a storage warehouse, and multiple offices. Business was booming and the future was promising.

Long Island, home to this business, is basically a thin strip of sand sticking out in the ocean. It's one hundred, twenty-two miles long and twenty-five miles wide. It contains every extreme micro-economy from hectic streets of Brooklyn to the luxurious Hamptons.

In hurricane season, it is not uncommon for hurricanes to hug the eastern coast of the United States as they travel north and then make a direct hit somewhere on Long Island. Hurricane Gloria which hit in 1985 was one such example. To be more specific for those who may not recall, Gloria was ranked by the National Weather Service as a Category 4 hurricane which ultimately left a path of over nine hundred million dollars in estimated damage, with Long Island being the place she made landfall for the second time.

The building I worked at was in the center of Long Island. Unfortunately for many, Hurricane Gloria hit the exact center. If you research the track of the storm, you will see where the eye passed directly over Islip Airport on Long Island. This business was in an industrial park next to that airport. The eye of the storm hovered exactly over the factory just as the dream had shown me. In even greater detail, and true to the dream, the roof peeled off right down to the metal. The boom of this business seemed to come to a screeching halt. We were officially out of business!

The owner was devastated. He had poured everything he had into the business and carried a huge debt load because of his financial investment. He was so distraught that he retreated to his home in California to gather his thoughts and to rest up from the trauma that had altered much of the East Coast.

Now, before I go on with this story, let me make this clear. I am no one special except that the same spirit that raised Christ from the dead lives in me.

This situation reminded me of lessons learned in my days at the Episcopal Church where the healing priest would occasionally minister. I was grateful to God for revealing how He allows every devoted Believer in Christ to minister to those in need. This enables me and anyone who carries His Holy Spirit to do amazing things.

While the owner was away, God's grace rested on the vision I held for this company and the owner. With an incredible team of people on board, we were able to not only get another roof put on, but to get the entire business up and running in an incredibly short period of time.

Jesus is the ultimate come back strategist. Through the power of the Holy Spirit, Jesus supplied the wisdom to deal with the contractors, the insurance company, and all that went into the restoration of the company. We were back in business and the owner was blown away, first literally and now figuratively!

I still give all the credit to Jesus as I am reminded that faith comes from hearing and hearing from the Word of God.

The dream entrusted to me had revealed what was going to happen and showed that He would give me the strength to stand and get the job done. I had nothing to fear and I had the encouragement from Holy Spirit that everything would come out ok. In the end, everything worked out and I received a nice pay raise too!

The next time you have a vivid dream that feels significant, pray and ask God to reveal if He has given it to you for the purpose of a warning or a message that may benefit you or someone in your circle of influence. The Bible is full of ordinary people like me who have the faith to believe for amazing things. I give God all the glory!

You can't make this up—but Jesus can!

Chapter 9
HARD LESSONS ON MY OWN

For I know my transgressions…

PSALM 51:3

Some years after Hurricane Gloria made her lasting mark, I determined it was time to make my own mark. I decided to start my own business. I knew better but I moved ahead without a clear green light from God. Pride and rebellion often go hand in hand. In retrospect, I never should have gone out on my own when God was not in the lead.

With that being said, God allows U-turns once we acknowledge Him and turn around. He has proven Himself to be the God of second chances over and over in my life.

My business took off initially but quickly began to lose momentum as I encountered many roadblocks. While I had always wanted to be out on my own professionally speaking, and that would eventually happen, I was about to learn the hard way that this was neither the time nor the place.

Let me try to make a long story a bit more concise for you. While the storage warehouse for the products associated with this new startup business was overflowing, the customer base was insufficient. In other words, I had more product to sell than customers to sell to. This was compounded by the fact that I had now accepted the risk of mounting bills related to rent on the warehouse, plus utilities and operational costs on top of personal expenses.

It now felt as if my business account was as low as my oil tank had once been at the old, tiny house. I had only a few inches of money left to try and conquer a mountain of debt. I was out of church at the time, so I had also stopped tithing.

During this time, my brother-in-law came for a visit to New York. While we were together, he introduced me to a pastor who came and prayed with me. I was drawn to a passage of Scripture that is not typically associated with tithing or giving back to God. It is found in the seventh chapter of Second Kings:

Now there were four men who were lepers at the

entrance to the gate. And they said to one another, "Why are we sitting here until we die? If we say, 'Let us enter the city,' the famine is in the city, and we shall die there. And if we sit here, we die also. So now come, let us go over to the camp of the Syrians. If they spare our lives we shall live, and if they kill us we shall but die." So they arose at twilight to go to the camp of the Syrians. But when they came to the edge of the camp of the Syrians, behold, there was no one there. For the Lord had made the army of the Syrians hear the sound of chariots and of horses, the sound of a great army, so that they said to one another, "Behold, the king of Israel has hired against us the kings of the Hittites and the kings of Egypt to come against us." So they fled away in the twilight and abandoned their tents, their horses, and their donkeys, leaving the camp as it was, and fled for their lives. And when these lepers came to the edge of the camp, they went into a tent and ate and drank, and they carried off silver and gold and clothing and went and hid them. Then they came back and entered another tent and carried off things from it and went and hid them. 2 Kings 7:3-8

A closer look into the story reveals an unexpected twist. When they arrived, they found the enemy camp abandoned. In the absence of the kings and the people of that land they ate like kings. Then they packed up the leftovers and brought them home to their starving friends.

My business account had dwindled to just under five hundred dollars. So, I decided to let the lepers in that story lead the way. I determined to take radical action instead of giving up the ship.

I launched my new season of faith by deciding to fast. For this time, I felt led to eat only one meal a day after sundown. This saved money on food, but it also held a deeper meaning. I was reminding myself and God that I trusted His provision more than my ability to produce.

My next step was to give away my last five hundred dollars to the pastor I had just met as the Lord prompted me to do.

Lastly, I was left to figure out a way to get out of the business I started. I knew I had to humble myself and find something else to do. I had a family to support and I had no idea what my next move would be.

At the end of thirty days, I received a call from a potential customer. They liked my products, but they already had an existing supplier and a loyalty to that business relationship. Suddenly, their current supplier could no longer meet their supply need. This unfortunate situation shifted an almost client into a large customer of mine. They requested a product shipment that yielded an initial profit of over forty-five thousand dollars!

The next order of business was to get out of the lease on the building I had rented to warehouse our products. There was about a year left and I wanted to get out without paying a penalty. I knew this was going to require another miracle. Just a day or two before Christmas that year, a man walked in the front door and said, "Is this building available for rent?" My mouth dropped open, as I felt my own Christmas miracle unfolding before my very own eyes and ears.

This man had started a hobby business selling baseball collectables out of his own home and he had outgrown that space. This business success left him in need of a building. Furthermore, he was hoping to find a place he could move into immediately. I felt as if a Christmas angel had been sent to deliver the best gift ever as that gentleman took over my lease right away. I was free!

There is still more to this amazing story. I invested in a friendship with this pastor and began attending the small church he pastored which met at a local funeral home. The church had very little money, so the budget could not fully support him. This left him tapping into his skill as a painter to support he and his family.

In the middle of this odd season in my own life, I faced an awkward situation. I intended to give a 10% tithe from that big customer order. That nearly fifty-thousand-dollar windfall added up to a gift of nearly five thousand dollars. That was a lot of money back in 1990! To many, it is still a lot of money.

I did not have a problem with giving the money away because I knew it was a gift honoring God for bailing me out of an impossible situation. It felt exciting and weird all at the same time to realize that the Lord had entrusted me with that money.

I began trying to envision the best way to give this gift to the pastor and the little church. Would I ask to meet him privately? Or would I just drop this check casually into the offering on a typical Sunday morning? I found myself in a place I had not navigated before and my imagination was working overtime. Maybe the pastor would think I was crazy or that the check was a fake. I didn't know what to expect.

God always has a plan and what He did next was marvelous. The pastor invited me over for dinner. They often served tuna casserole. Although I hate tuna casserole, I ate it out of gratitude and a deep desire to not to insult them. As we enjoyed this poor man's dinner, I sat in amazement of the five-thousand-dollar check lurking in my pocket. I had asked the Lord to set up the right moment for me to bless this faithful family. Praying silently while gagging on the tuna casserole, "Jesus, I need your help."

Just then, the conversation turned to teeth and dental care. The pastor mentioned casually that his wife needed extensive dental care and it was going to cost five thousand dollars. He had no idea how to find the money. I may not be the smartest man in the world, but I know my que.

I reached in my pocket and offered an unexpected answer to their situation. The word stunned does not do justice to the look on their faces. The Holy Ghost laughter that ensued was nothing short of incredible. Someday, I will meet them again. Whether on earth or in Heaven, I sure am looking forward to reliving this story.

It has been said by many that you cannot out-give God. This story still reminds me that His strategies, timing, and purposes are higher than mine. I learned in that season to invite Jesus to sit at the head of the table when making personal and professional decisions. While this story ended miraculously, I learned my lesson. I am no fool and I did not want to make the same painful mistakes again in the future!

If you are about to make a life-altering decision, such as the decision to go into business for yourself, bring God into the discussion proactively and follow His lead in all that you do. You will be blessed, and your peace will be multiplied.

You can't make this up—but Jesus can!

Chapter 10
MESSENGER BIRD

Do all things without grumbling or questioning.

PHILIPPIANS 2:13

Our time on Long Island, the only home I had ever known, was coming to a close. The Lord began speaking to me about Florida. I was not interested in the least. My situation reminded me of Jacob when famine struck, and he was forced to go to Egypt. All my efforts in New York were spiraling downward and moving was becoming a harsh reality. Long Island had been in a tremendous decade of Revival from the late Seventies to this time, which was the late Eighties. The Revival had come to an end and it was God's timing for us to go.

In the meantime, it seemed as if I was cursed at every turn. Everything I touched seemed to be turning to dust. Looking back now, I realize that it was largely my fault. The Lord was doing His part in leading, but I did not want to be led. When we get in the way of God's leading, the type of resistance I was feeling in this season begins to manifest.

Our God is a jealous God. By that, I mean that He is eager for us to get our agenda out of the way so He can move in our lives unhindered. God is also pure love. So unlike human jealousy, which is born out of selfishness, even His jealousy is pure and rooted in love. He is the most trustworthy, loving, and wise Father that we could ever entrust our lives and plans to.

As a teen, I worked on a dairy farm. Cows love grass, especially lush, green grass. Yet, when we would open a new pasture with abundant grass, the young calves would just stand frozen looking at it. They all but refused to go in. I had to poke the young calves with a stick to get them moving toward their grassy field of provision. Once they were in, they would run and jump for joy. In the same gentle way, God was nudging me toward a new opportunity. But like those calves, I found myself standing, staring, and not moving. Wow, back then I never thought that I would expose my weakness by comparing myself to a young calf, but I guess it is too late now.

Finally, I did obey. This meant going ahead of my family to seek a new job and a new place to live. I will admit that the grass did not initially look more lush or green in this new land. I had no connections. I drove countless hours to a place where my family knew no one—Florida.

My expectations grew strong as I traveled. I thought since I now obeyed, everything would be fixed at once. I was about to learn another powerful lesson. The process of restoration can often take more time than we wish to sacrifice. I wanted another immediate miracle, like the time when the guy walked in and took over my business lease. But this was going to be a different season.

After having my pride crushed as I bounced between jobs, I was finally hired at a Mazda dealership. Did I happen to mention that I hate selling cars? I was on a fast track toward humility as my business had failed, leading me to spend my days courting customers who may or may not buy a vehicle.

Little did I realize that God was crafting a sort of bootcamp for me that would pay many dividends in my future business life. Despite what it looked like, God was not finished working. It just felt that way to me because failure is a hard pill to swallow. Yet failure is not the opposite of success. I was learning that it is all a part of our greater success, as God does not waste one single life lesson.

It's hard to see God's plan when you are "up to your neck in alligators" to borrow a Florida term. Car salespeople work six days per week, often twelve hours per day, receiving insults from customers much of the time. Ethics and honesty in that business often go unrewarded.

There I was selling new cars while driving an old, shabby Honda Civic with over 200,000 miles. To add insult to injury, the car had no air conditioning and I was now living in the Florida heat and humidity. Even though the Lord was leading the way, I grumbled and complained much like the children of Israel as they wandered in the desert. I had studied the Bible enough to be able to imagine their grumbling and to find humor as my behavior seemed to echo theirs. Had God brought me out to this desert to die? I mean seriously, I had experienced miracle upon miracle as my own business came to a close in the home state I had grown to love. Now, here I was living in a state with bugs larger than my smallest children. The oppressive heat and humidity reminded me moment by moment just how much had changed in my life. I felt like a failure—a hot and sweaty failure.

As I mentioned earlier, I loved to pick up hitchhikers as one of my mission fields. Some would consider that practice dangerous, but I was not afraid. Fear is crushed when we follow the Lord's voice. While this may not be everyone's God-assignment, if He asks you to give someone a ride, He will cover you in that situation. It was a great opportunity to share Jesus.

One night while coming home in the sweltering heat, I saw a hitchhiker. I was in a bad mood, so I did not stop. I just drove past him as I continued to sulk in self-pity. Not long after that, my car stalled at a red light. No matter how hard I tried, it would not restart. Those old Hondas have a timing belt and when it breaks, it can do major damage to the engine. That's exactly what happened to me. I had ignored God's timing with the person who needed a ride. Now, the tables turned as I became the guy in need of my own Good Samaritan. Can you see the irony? The situation provided me a much needed attitude adjustment!

From this point on, the public bus became my only way to work. What I would have given for God to bring that old car back to life. Because of the bus lines, my commute went from thirty minutes to an hour and a half one way. To make matters worse, I had to ride on two buses coming and going from work. My twelve-hour day just jumped to an unthinkable fifteen hours. You can probably imagine what this did for my mood and my morale. Where was God and why was this happening to me?

One morning, I was waiting at a stop between the first and second bus routes. It was ninety-five degrees with ninety-five percent humidity as I stood baking in the sun. For those who have not spent much time in Florida in the summer, believe me when I tell you that this combination made the temperature index feel well over one hundred degrees.

I could not control my frustration any longer, so I looked toward Heaven as I declared to the Lord, "things can't get any worse!"

Despite the traits I do not love about that state, Florida does have many beautiful birds and a vast amount of vegetation upon which they love to feed. There is a specific variety of bush with dark blue berries that make the color of a blueberry appear pale. These berries are not edible for humans. On this particular morning, while standing at the bus stop, I was wearing a button-down shirt with a pocket on the upper left side. With the heat and humidity, the shirt was limp with sweat and the pocket was drooping half open.

One of those beautiful, exotic Florida birds must

have feasted on a breakfast of one of those dark blue-berry-like bushes that day.

At the exact moment I was looking up at the sky and uttered the last word of compliant to the Lord, as the word "worse" was flowing from my lips, one of these birds decided to relieve himself of his digested breakfast with a direct hit into my shirt pocket. The accuracy of his aim was as if a laser guided Tomahawk missile had been expertly delivered from an F15 fighter pilot.

As my seeming bad luck would have it, I was on my way to work rather than heading home after a long day. So, I now had a blue stain in my pocket that would act as a continual reminder of this terrible moment all day long as I tried to look professional for customers!

All during my workday, I was forced to make a choice. Do I tell the truth, or do I go along with everyone's assumption that a blue ballpoint pen had exploded in my pocket? I chose the latter. Leaked ink felt a bit less humiliating than bird missiles. I had started out resisting God's prompting to help the guy in need of a ride and now I was lying about a stupid stain.

It did not take long to put the whole matter into perspective. My bad attitude desperately needed an adjustment. In the midst of my frustration and emotional pain, I had become a sweaty brat quicker than the Florida sun could bake my New York skin.

God never leaves or forsakes us. Despite this timeless truth, I had forgotten His goodness and the need to remain grateful in all circumstances. Instead of focusing on what God was attempting to do in my life by opening this new land of opportunity, I chose to focus on what I did not have. That one simple decision landed me in the mire of self-pity and self-focus.

From then on, whenever I would find myself in difficult situations, I would remind myself that only one thing had greater accuracy that that bird's aim at my shirt pocket. God's strategic wisdom and His love for His sons and daughters is far more accurate. That revelation saw me through many challenging seasons, including an experience of being homeless. Through it all, I can proudly proclaim—God can be trusted in every season of life!

You can't make this up—but Jesus can!

Chapter 11
FASTER THAN A RACEHORSE

Fear not, stand firm, and see the salvation of
the LORD, which he will work for you today.

Exodus 14:13

It took a while, but Florida did grow on me as I allowed
God to recalibrate my outlook. Little by little, things became easier.

One day at the auto dealership, God provided another faith building opportunity. I was positioned to
learn a new concept for difficult situations. God was
teaching me how to view a perceived problem as an
opportunity to build my faith and glorify God.

R.W. Schambach always used to say that you don't
have a problem as long as you have faith in God. This
powerful man of God had come to understand that
God has a solution for every problem we encounter.
The key is looking to Him instead of our own understanding.

It was the last day of the month. My rent was due, and my car sales were not enough to cover my bills. The once-monthly payroll often left me and the other sales associates with too much month remaining at the end of our paychecks.

I was standing in front of the dealership with another salesperson. An elderly woman and a younger woman drove up in an old, white Jeep Cherokee. They proceeded to park directly in front of me. We took turns waiting on customers and it was the other salesperson's time to go. She looked at me and said, "You can take this one. They are not going to buy anything."

I did not see them as buyers either, but I had nothing to lose, so I walked over and introduced myself. To set the scene completely, I needed one thousand dollars for the rent, and this was the last day of the month. The average commission on a typical car ranged from two to three hundred dollars. At that rate, it would have taken three or more individual sales to meet my current need for rent money.

The elderly woman was wearing a necklace that immediately captured my attention. I assumed it had to be costume jewelry. It was large and flashy. I can still recall the outline of a horse in silver, approximately four inches wide by three inches high. I was certain that the single stone had to be a huge cubic zirconia instead of a real diamond.

She introduced herself and wasted no time getting down to business. To my amazement, she bypassed the customary chit chat and leaped ahead to the bottom line as if she had no time to waste. As it turned out, she really didn't have much time.

I was shocked at the words that came out of her mouth. "I am going in for brain surgery tomorrow and if I don't make it out alive, I want to leave something for my great-granddaughter to remember me by. She is about to turn sixteen. What can you show me?"

Talk is often cheap, so I decided to put the situation to the test.

We had a gorgeous, special edition Mazda Miata on the lot at the time, a sleek, two-seater convertible. This model was quite rare, and the dealership only had one in stock. It was black with a red leather interior and wire alloy wheels. If you are not familiar with the Mazda line of cars, this little roadster has been a best-seller for decades.

I escorted her over to the car and without any hesitation she said, "I'll take it." I had just sold a car in record time! She then added, "I'll take the removable hardtop too." The hardtop added an extra twenty-five hundred dollars to her total tab.

Still not sure if this was really happening, I asked how she would like to pay. Again, without any hesitation, she reached in her purse and handed me an American Express credit card that boasted an unlimited credit limit. It was beginning to sink in. This was the real deal.

I don't recall the exact amount of the sale, but it came to somewhere around twenty-seven thousand dollars. I do remember that my commission was just over one thousand dollars, the threshold I needed to not get evicted by my landlord. My rent was paid.

By the way, the horse necklace was real diamonds and precious metals. I had just sold a convertible in a quick minute to the owner of an Ocala, Florida farm that specialized in breeding champion racehorses.

People talk about God showing up in the eleventh hour, meaning when time is almost up on our miracle. Once again, I was blessed, humbled, and reminded of a powerful truth that is more precious than diamonds or platinum. God is faithful.

You can't make this up—but Jesus can!

Chapter 12
3,2,1 ... LIFTOFF

And let us not neglect our meeting together,
as some people do, but encourage one another...
HEBREWS 10:25 (NLT)

Within thirty minutes of landing in Florida, I found a church. It was my top priority, even above finding a job. I passed by a church sign on the roadside and I was drawn to the name, Full Gospel Assembly. I needed a full experience with God, not a partial one, so I decided to check it out. The church lived up to the word full in its name. This Body of Believers and its leadership believed in the gifts of the spirit and I was thankful for that. I credit my time there as a key to my overall spiritual development. I ended up staying there for the fifteen years I was in Florida.

Pastor Richard was an interesting guy. Some would say you don't need to be a rocket scientist to be a pastor, but Richard ironically was both. He had recently retired from his full time career working for the space center at Cape Canaveral. As one nod to his years spent in that industry, he was in a key development and leadership position for the Apollo Mission that put men on the moon. Like me, he was also a pilot, so we learned that we had a lot in common.

Before Richard's family moved to Florida, they lived in Pennsylvania. Our sojourn to this southern-most state out of the northeast was another key thing we held in common.

As a young boy he used to shine Finis Dakes's shoes. Finis Dake created the Dake Annotated Reference Bible and was the author of God's Plan for Man. Dake was a notable pastor, Bible scholar, and teacher whose life spanned from 1902-1987.

Pastor Richard's father had owned a shoe repair store where Dake used to come in to have his shoes repaired and shined. As his shoes were being tended to, Dake and Richard's father would debate Scripture. It has been stated that Dake had the Bible memorized backwards and forwards. Pastor Richard said you could give him a verse and he could tell you corresponding book and chapter. Richard said Dake could also quote a passage verbatim after having been given the book, chapter, and verse.

Pastor Richard's father could hold his own with Dake. His wisdom on Scripture was way beyond his education and upbringing. Dake would ask him how he knew so much about Scripture. Pastor's father would just reply, "Finis, you have theology, but I have knee-ology," indicating that his time spent on his knees with the Lord had yielded revelation and knowledge and wisdom.

In later years, my Dad who was fading to Alzheimer's roomed with Pastor Richard's father in the same health care facility. I am thankful for exposure to such great leaders of the faith during my time in Florida, a season of my life that yielded a deeper level of spiritual maturity and knowledge of the Word of God.

You can't make this up—but Jesus can!

Chapter 13
ONE DOOR CLOSES AND ANOTHER OPENS

The steps of a man are established by the LORD,
when he delights in his way.

PSALM 37:23

After my time in the car business finally ended, God was preparing to put my boot-camp-learning into practice. For a long time, every job interview seemed to end the same way. The interview process would come down to me and one other person and always ended up with the other person getting the position.

My wife had convinced me to take a leap of faith and quit the car business. She said I should just go for it. Shortly thereafter, I was out on another interview. Once again, it was a position I felt fully qualified for, but history repeated itself as the other guy won out.

I pulled out of the parking lot dealing with the rejection and anxiety knowing that I had already left the car business and now had no income. As I rounded the corner of that business, I saw another company on the main road. Since I had multiple copies of my resume, I thought to myself, "What do I have to lose? Nothing. I am already dressed for an interview, so I will give it a shot."

The business was the largest and oldest industrial laundry in the Southeast, headquartered in Atlanta. This was their Orlando branch which mainly served the booming restaurant and tourist industry.

As I walked in the door, I felt I had time-traveled back to 1950. Solid wood paneling, old-school fluorescent lights, and aged oak desks all contributed to the retro vibe. This was long before retro was back in vogue. The receptionist who greeted me was also a perfect fit. I assumed she was in her sixties, as her style included a teased, bouffant hairstyle, cat-eye glasses with rhinestones that came to a point, and an antique necklace.

I politely asked if they had any openings in their sales department. She said she believed so as she requested my resume. I promptly handed her the one I had ready to go.

As I was about to leave, I asked how long she had been working for this company. She said she was coming up on fifty years. I said, "Wow, amazing! How did you do it?" She said, "Well this place has its problems, but I figured if I went anywhere else, they would have their problems too so I might as well stay where I am." At that moment, she felt full of wisdom and tenacity.

I was offered the job and the story quickly got even better. The first order I secured was the largest non-restaurant order ever placed. The next five years of my work began with that wave of restoration.

In a short time, I was blessed with a promotion to sales manager over the entire state of Florida. The job enabled me and my family to purchase our own home in Florida and gain a more stable financial foundation as the restoration continued.

In retrospect, it was one of the best jobs I ever had. Along with financial stability, I also felt a vast increase in my quality of life. With co-workers I genuinely enjoyed worked with, this was a complete package deal. I have remained in touch with some of the salespeople that worked on my team. Together, we set a sales record that had not been reached by anyone else in the company's one-hundred-year history. I gave God's goodness all the credit.

After five years, despite a great run at this job, I felt prompted to respond to an ad for a sales manager position at Grainger, the largest industrial supply company in the United States. My wife questioned why I would rock the boat when it was going so well. That was a fair question that I couldn't answer at the time. I just felt compelled.

In the meantime, we had a meeting with the president of my then-current company. There were rumors of a sale. At a breakfast meeting, a few of us decided to ask the direct question, "Is the company up for sale?"

With a firm resounding "No," he said our jobs were all secure. This guy did not make himself easy to trust. He claimed to be a Christian, but this Sunday School teacher cursed like a drunken sailor. This scenario fueled my desire to move on.

I ended up taking the position with Grainger and shortly after, all my former peers were terminated in a downsizing and the company was sold. I escaped just in time. As happy as I was there, the position at Grainger turned out to be even better.

Not every story has a happy ending. When I started with Grainger, after only a couple of weeks, I hit a wall. My daughter needed a chaperone for a school field trip to Universal Studios. Having always been a workaholic, the thought of asking for time off at a new job seemed out of the question. That character flaw and misplaced commitment to work that often overshadowed my own family has led to most of my regrets. I had already missed my son Michael's big catch at a football game because I opted to work late on that irreplaceable day.

This time, much to my daughter's surprise, I decided to do it differently. I took a deep breath and asked my new boss for the day off. To my surprise, he said yes with this comment, "I wish I took more time off when my kids were younger." The balance between earning a living and spending time with your kids haunts many a parent. Still, during the day of the field trip, I made one call to the office to check-in. I was devastated to find out that the very night before that the boss's son had taken his own life with a pistol in the backyard.

Jobs come, and careers go. Days spent making money should not be allowed to overshadow the lasting impact our neglect can have on our families, health, and peace of mind.

My heart broke over this leader's loss while it simultaneously caused me to take stock of my own life. I had healthy children, a new job on the horizon, and a fresh opportunity to recalibrate my priorities. I was a blessed man.

You can't make this up—but Jesus can!

Chapter 14
DRIVE-BY TITHE

Give, and it will be given to you. Good measure,
pressed down, shaken together, running over, will be
put into your lap. For with the measure you use it will
be measured back to you.

LUKE 6:38

The Lord has an incredible sense of humor. When my family and I were living in Orlando, Florida, there was a unique financial experience. At this point in my walk of faith, I was leaning more on the legalistic side, but it was based on faith and what I thought God expected. I was doing my best with what I had learned up to that point in my life.

My wife and I were not exactly on the same page when it came to the Biblical practice of giving a percentage back to God from all that you earn, known as tithing. Money was tight so when our tax return came in, we ended up having a disagreement. I wanted to tithe down to the penny, but she did not. Rather than turn a disagreement into a dragged-out fight, I simply turned toward Heaven and said to God, "I can't deal with this, you talk to her."

I still recall the tax return being $2,349 and some change. Since calculating a ten-percent tithe is easy, I figured $234.90 should do it. I did not have her agreement.

Orlando had some rough neighborhoods, but the area we lived in was considered very safe. Even petty crimes were rare. At the time we had an old Dodge Caravan, a practical vehicle shaped like a shoebox with a large hatch and a huge window in the rear. It was new and represented part of the financial recovery we were experiencing. We always parked in the driveway since the garage was full of bicycles and kid's stuff.

The same night that we had this argument over whether to tithe on our tax return, someone drove through the neighborhood with a pellet gun and shot out that hatch window. None of the other windows, not even the front windshield, were touched. Unfortunately, none of it was covered by my insurance policy. When the auto glass company came to replace the window, the bill came to $234.

At this point in my walk with God, I could have easily decided this was a judgment against us for arguing over whether to give the exact amount back to God after receiving that tax return. Today, I don't believe God was punishing us. Rather, I have come to know this about His Divine nature. He loves a cheerful giver. In fact, He can honor our obedience down to the penny, and often gives back far more than we could ever give to Him or His Kingdom.

I want to leave you with this message. God deserves our first fruits from our labor. To be more accurate, He owns it all as He allows us to become good stewards. Our Father wants to operate in power in our daily lives by meeting every need as our ultimate provider. One of the best ways to show God that we have faith in His ability to provide for us is to give a portion of our earnings, time, and talents back to Him for His purposes.

Giving should be a part of every Christian's life and we should not hesitate to walk in generosity. It does not boil down to a mathematical calculation like the Pharisees practiced. I now realize that He owns everything, and it is an honor to gift back to Him in whatever way He leads.

You can't make this up—but Jesus can!

Chapter 15
HORSES IN THE RAINFOREST

The leaves of the tree were for the healing of the nations.
REVELATION 22:2

As my wife and I approached our twenty-fifth wedding anniversary, we began talking about taking a special vacation. I was in favor of going back to Hawaii, the place where we spent our honeymoon. Once you venture beyond the overrun tourist areas, it is one of the most beautiful places on earth.

I have great memories from that first trip to the islands where I taught her how to drive a standard shift on a rental car. We visited the Arizona Memorial and took in all the sights. We were on an extremely tight budget but somehow, we were able to make it happen.

For this trip, her pick was Costa Rica. Another couple was going, and she wanted to do a joint trip. In the end, she won out. Wives are usually gifted in that way.

My son Michael had visited Costa Rica on a surfing trip and raved about its beauty.

I gave in to her choice because I was just glad to be getting away. I was in a high-pressure job and the thought of any exotic getaway felt perfect. I was also looking forward to catching up on some much needed Bible study time. I had been wanting an English Standard Version (ESV) of the Bible. At the last minute, I picked up a copy and tossed it into my backpack as we headed off to the airport. I left it in the box to protect it during travel.

This trip was bare bones in terms of planning. With just the airline reservation, the first hotel night, and the rental car. Everything else was an open-ended adventure. No structure. Just a car, a map, and the open country.

Many of the backwoods restaurants were in local homes. They add a patio with extra tables onto their house and presto, native Costa Rica residents were in the restaurant business. Some of the best seafood I have ever eaten was served in these roadside venues, fresh and cooked to order using Grandma's favorite recipes.

One night, we stayed at a hostel that was originally

a National Geographic basecamp. It was located at the base of Mt. Arenal, an active volcano. We slept in front of a huge picture window and watched the orange flares of the molten lava shoot into the air. The next day, we relaxed in the river below with its hot-tub-temperature water as the pumice stone cleansed and buffed our skin naturally. Even Hawaii would have a tough time competing with that experience.

One evening as we headed to find a hotel, we passed a sign that advertised horseback riding through the rainforest. Without hesitation, I pulled off the road to the shack behind the sign. You guessed it. In a land where homes become restaurants, shacks could double as corporate offices. We talked with the owner, but it was too late in the day to take the tour, so we agreed to meet up in the morning.

Early the next day we arrived anxious to add this excursion to our list of experiences. The trip consisted of an hour and a half horseback ride followed by traveling on foot for another hour to the top of the mountain where a waterfall awaited us.

Howling monkeys and wild parrots with their long red tails escorted us up the mountain. Near the top, our tour guide, Vic, pointed out the leafcutter ants marching in disciplined order, each with their own slice of a leaf to bring to their nest. Vic also pointed out leaves used for medicinal purposes; one for headache, another for stomach troubles, and so on. His knowledge of botanicals was extensive and impressive.

As we crested the top of the mountain, we stopped for a much needed rest. What happened next was unusual, to say the least. With a half-joking opening line, Vic said, "Now that you are exhausted, you are my captive audience. I am going to share my story with you." He went on to explain how he had promised God that he would share his story with everyone he guided on these tours.

He regaled us with a personal story of a time when brain cancer had threatened his life, finally winning. He had died after being told that his disease was no longer treatable! This was after chemo, radiation, and surgery had collectively failed him. Here is a glimpse into the story Vic shared with us that day:

When I arrived in Heaven, Jesus greeted me. He explained that my house was not finished yet and that I needed to go back.

At this point, I should have asked how long he was dead. But I was so wrapped up in this story that I didn't think of it. I was frozen to every word. He went on to tell us how his story was documented by the hospital where he was treated during this ordeal.

He went on to explain that the doctors told him, because of the chemo and radiation, he would be unable to father any children. In this culture, he explained that it would have been highly unlikely that any woman would have ever chosen to love and accept him. This most likely meant a death sentence to his dreams, after the death sentence to his very life.

Concluding his story, Vic removed his ball cap to reveal a head that looked like a road map. Scars were running in different directions from the multiple surgeries he had endured on his brain. Up to this point, I was somewhat skeptical, as I had never met anyone who had been raised from the dead. After looking at the scars, I was convinced that he had to be telling the truth. He invited us to contact the doctors and the hospital to fact-check his story.

It took bravery to capture an audience and boldness to share his God story with tourists from all walks of life. I have always admired his tenacity. I still recall how a few members of the group were annoyed and upset that he chose to share his story. As a Believer in Christ, I still appreciate how his story fueled my faith. I also carry gratitude for that moment, knowing full well that if I had not known Jesus up to that point in my life, chances are strong that I would have met our Healing Savior for the first time right then and there.

We headed down the mountain back to the spot where the horses were waiting. All the others mounted up and went on ahead, leaving just Vic and me behind.

We talked about the Lord all the way down the trail. Jesus came into the midst of our conversation with a tangible power that reminded me of the story of the Disciples on the road to Damascus following the Resurrection.

Vic spoke perfect English with eloquence and wisdom which led me to believe that he might have an international education. Since Spanish was the primary language there, I asked what country he studied in. I was amazed when this accomplished man told me that he had never been out of Costa Rica. It became clear that the Lord had taught him and equipped him with a powerful testimony.

What happened next was like icing on the cake. Vic told me he preached on occasion. I asked if that was in English or Spanish. He told me many times in Spanish, but that he liked the challenge of preaching in English. I asked if there was anything I could do for him. He replied that while he had a Spanish Bible, he really wanted an English Bible. With a sneaky smile cracking from the corner of my mouth, I reached over my right shoulder, unzipped my backpack, and pulled out the brand new, boxed Revised Standard English Bible I had packed at the beginning of the trip. There was nothing else in my backpack except the Bible. As I handed it to him, I said, "Will this work?"

We laughed so hard that I thought we would fall off our horses! I have never forgotten that miracle man. I can only hope that he has practically worn out that Bible preaching and sharing his amazing testimony.

By the way, Vic is now married and has two beautiful daughters. He is still giving tours on the same mountain and can be reached by googling Vic-Tours Costa Rica. As I was writing this book, I reached out to him and asked for the honor and permission to include his story.

I am sure he would love to give you a tour and share his story in person. If you make your way to his beautiful country and up his mountain, ask him to show you that Bible and the scars of victory on his head.

You can't make this up—but Jesus can!

Philip found himself at Azotus...

ACTS 8:40

I hope that I will never lose my wonder for how God works. Nearing the end of my stay in Florida, I gathered each Friday night with some local youth for a time of prayer and worship. We would pray for members of the church, pray for revelation, or anything else that came to our minds and hearts. We had no agenda except our collective desire to usher in the presence of God.

The stage spanned nearly the entire width of the room; approximately fifty feet, with stairs that also extended almost the exact width of that massive stage.

One memorable night, we were worshiping and praising as usual while pre-recorded music created the soundtrack for this time together with the Father. I still recall positioning myself on the far-right side of the stage near the edge. I cannot tell you exactly how long we prayed and worshiped, but it felt like a long time. I wish I could remember more about that night. But I can't recall who or what I felt prompted to pray for at the time. All I know is that something happened which I have never forgotten. Despite no recollection of getting up and moving about during this time of prayer, when the time finally concluded, I finally opened my eyes only to find that I had somehow mysteriously relocated to the complete opposite side of the stage—stage left.

For many, this may feel like a random testimony without a direct or clear point. Perhaps that is the point. God is full of mystery, wonder, and supernatural power. He is often moving in us and through us in ways far beyond our comprehension—or even beyond our current awareness. Invite His presence to saturate the atmosphere of your heart. His wonderful ways will keep the wonder in our hearts.

When we wholeheartedly seek to usher in the presence of the living God, we should not be shocked when signs and wonders follow. I have learned to seek God more than I seek miracles because I never want to fall into the trap of worshiping what God can do instead of worshiping God simply for who He is.

You can't make this up—but Jesus can!

Chapter 17
START YOUR ENGINES!

The fire had not had any power over the bodies of those men. The hair of their heads was not singed, their cloaks were not harmed, and no smell of fire had come upon them.

DANIEL 3:27

Of all that I have been privileged to witness so far in my life, this story ranks near the top. It made national news and can still be witnessed online.

At the time it happened, I knew it was profound. Little did I know just how powerful it would prove to be in the future.

I was still working for Grainger as the Sales Manager over the Orlando District. The company was enjoying a historic growth period at the time as God poured out His blessing in amazing ways.

My Corporate Manager had a lot of influence in the company. He made the bold, and expensive, marketing decision to enter the world of NASCAR. He proposed that the company should sponsor a driver in our newly formed Craftsman Truck Series. These marketing decisions often cost sponsoring companies tens of millions of dollars.

The decision was made to take this marketing risk. The driver selected was Greg Biffle, and the race team was Roush Racing. There was a buzz in the air among the Grainger employees, making this a great time to be working for this cutting-edge company.

After completing several initial races, it came time for the big one—Daytona Beach, aptly named for the beach where it had its humble beginnings long before a track existed. This would be the first time ever that trucks would compete at what has become one of the most famous racetracks in the world.

The key to using stock car racing as a marketing tool is to connect with potential future customers in a sport that is important to them. At that time, our broad customer base was made up of many NASCAR fans, making this a worthwhile gamble for Grainger. The racing world is not unlike professional football or baseball, boasting countless fans with drivers they loved and drivers they loved to hate. It was good, competitive fun.

Grainger's presence as an official sponsor gave us a strategic means of connecting with current and potential customers on their turf; the place where their favorite drivers and teams raced. We would hold large customer events at each race in hospitality tents outside the track. Food would be served while the fans could meet the drivers, get autographs, have priceless photographs taken, and swap stories with other fans.

My administrative assistant at the time was a woman named Kim. Kim had been raised in a family-founded Pentecostal Church in New Jersey, but she had later moved to Florida. Kim's spiritual status was not unlike many Christians. Somewhere along the way, she got hurt and took on a negative view of the church. Her story highlights how our adversary looks for ways to blame God when people fail us. If we are not careful, we will end up falling into this trap of blaming God ourselves.

It is a natural human tendency to shy away from the things we believe have wounded us. This can originate in a belief that everything that happens is God's will, based on the sovereignty of God. The truth is that God created us with free will and some choose to use that free will for selfish, destructive behaviors against others. The enemy comes in and blames God. He whispers in your ears, "how could a God of love let that happen to you? If He really loved you, and if He was real, He wouldn't stand by and let that happen to you." Sounds logical, right? Nothing could be further from the truth. God was, is, and will always be love. God, however, does not manipulate or micro-manage human choice.

Whenever the subject of Church or Jesus would come up in the office, Kim would often say, "Someday, I'll go back." I tried to not be pushy or insistent, but I carried a burden for Kim in her disillusionment. The Holy Spirit is gentle. I would mostly focus on sharing personal stories of God's goodness and faithfulness, while secretly interceding for her to my Father.

While Kim went on for several years saying, "Someday," God was not ultimately concerned about her return to church. His true aim was to draw her back into intimate fellowship with Himself.

Just a simple side note here: never put off to tomorrow what God wishes to do in your heart today.

In Romans Chapter 2 it says that it is the goodness of God that brings us to repentance. I am not a fan of that word repentance in certain circumstances and this is one of them. Literally, it means to change direction and specifically our mind or thought pattern. We behave based on what we think. If we believe God brings bad things upon us, then we act accordingly. We must renew our minds to understand that He is a good Father and loves us dearly. When we experience bad things, it can be hard to keep that in mind, leading many to become distant and detached.

On race day, Kim and two other assistants were working in the hospitality tent. This included meeting customers and potential customers while distributing gift bags and capturing valuable contact information. As the race began, I made my way to our seats along with our guests while Kim and the others wrapped up things at the tent. As they headed to their seats, the race had already begun.

The set up at Daytona during this time was that you could walk to your seats along the fence which separated the track from the seating area. Once the race was underway, pedestrians like Kim were literally inches away from the race cars—or in this case trucks— moving at speeds up to 200 mph.

Television cannot do justice to the experience of being at that track in person. My seat was about twenty-five rows up from the fence. I watched as Kim and the two others walked along the fence, intent on meeting up with us and taking their seats. Just at the point when they were approaching directly in front of our seats, the unthinkable happened.

Racer Geoff Bodine was behind the wheel of one of the trucks as the drivers flew around the track, side by side. All at once, trucks collided, and Geoff's truck became completely airborne. As it took to the air, the bottom of the truck came up against the fence. The devastating crash began just a few feet behind where Kim and the others were walking. With the onset of the collision behind them, they had no idea what was heading their way.

To see this miraculous event for yourself, go online to YouTube.co key search using keywords: Geoff Bodine, Truck Race, 2000, Truck Crash. Multiple videos are available which captured the miracle as it unfolded. It is graphic, so please view it first before making the decision on whether to share it with others.

If you watch this archived video, you will see that ten trucks were caught up in this collision. Pay attention to the footage where you will see an official in a yellow shirt at the spot where the truck first hits the fence. Directly below them are the three assistants, and Kim was the one closest to the fence.

Just as the airborne truck came in line with them, the fuel tank ruptured, spraying high octane fuel all over the trio. Racing fuel is vastly different from the fuel that runs your car or truck. It is specifically formulated for racing and is highly flammable. Almost instantly, as the fuel combined with oxygen in the atmosphere and a spark from the shearing metal against the fence, the fuel tank ignited.

From where I was seated, I could feel the intense heat of the fire as it blazed out of control. Kim and her co-workers were engulfed in the middle of the fireball to the point they were no longer visible. My heart sank as I battled to resist my first thought that they had to be dead, burned alive. I could not imagine how anyone could possibly escape this explosion.

Almost as fast as it ignited, the fireball dissipated. To our astonishment, they were standing there stunned but unharmed. My team and I ran to them immediately. There were only a couple of minor bruises from flying metal to serve as a physical reminder of what had just taken place.

Even more miraculous, their shirts were soaked in racing fuel and yet, they did not ignite. This detail defied the natural rules of how fire operates. We headed quickly to the infield hospital where the soaked clothing had to be immediately cut off to keep the volatile liquid from burning their skin.

By the way, this is the first time that Kim had ever attended a stock car race! Her initiation made NAS-CAR history.

The race shut down for hours. Further inspection revealed just how incredibly miraculous this day really was. Bodine's truck had completely ripped down the fence just inches away from where Kim was walking. Geoff Bodine suffered multiple injuries including broken bones, but he fully recovered.

Not a hair on Kim's head was singed! She walked away with a fuel-soaked shirt and a few small bruises and memories to last a lifetime.

God had just performed a miracle and it was all captured on video as a timeless reminder of His mercy and power. What a wonderful feeling it is to be delivered from disaster unharmed. He is truly our protector. "Behold, he who keeps Israel will neither slumber nor sleep." Psalm 121:4

The best take-away from this harrowing ordeal is that Kim's relationship with the Lord was restored. Kim returned to the Lord and to church to fellowship alongside her husband and their fellow Believers. I know from personal communication that she and her husband committed to raise their children to know Jesus. They went on to develop multiple successful businesses and to enjoy their children and several precious grandchildren.

When I contacted Kim to ask her permission to share her story, she messaged me back immediately. She and her husband were just discussing the event after watching the most recent 2020 Daytona 500 the weekend before I had reached out.

Ryan Newman had just survived a horrible wreck that occurred during that recent race. Not since Geoff Bodine's historic crash—and Kim's historic miracle—had there been such a wreck. This prompted sportscasters to revisit and replay the famous ten-truck wreck from twenty years ago!

Unaware of this timing, I had reached out just as the Lord had prompted her and her husband to remember and remain grateful for how her life had been spared that day.

You can't make this up—but Jesus can! Times Two!!

Chapter 18
TIME TO GO

I have commanded the ravens to feed you there.

1 KINGS 17:4

I worked with Grainger for nine years. During that time, the Lord poured out blessing upon blessing in my life. Life was full at work and away from the office. I was active in the church where I especially enjoyed teaching Sunday School to young adults. This season became a reminder that God does indeed restore, as what was lost in New York was now being made new.

I have come to know a Father who often restores above and beyond what has been formerly lost. I found myself not only with a great job but with a career that promised millionaire status and early retirement by age fifty-five.

With God's wisdom and blessing, the district I had been asked to lead soared from the bottom third in the company to the top three percent. From this mountain-top executive position, I had a premium view of my future. I truly believed I would ride this wave of success to the end of my career and straight into early retirement. There was only one problem. Things were about to change.

I remember being in a meeting with my peers in Chicago. It was a large auditorium with stage-like seating. I was at the top of my career, and with gratitude to God, I knew Who put me there. That is when the same God who launched me onto this glorious mountain top began to speak. While sitting there, I heard that still small voice I had come to know and respect. The Lord spoke softly, "Your time here is finished." What? I could not be hearing Him correctly. So, I tuned in closely as He continued to speak, "Your time here is finished."

"You have got to be kidding me," I thought to myself. I just got here, and I had settled into my comfortable plan to stay on this career path! Despite my best plans, it was not to be.

To be truly honest with you now, just as I had to be with myself at that time, I was sensing a stirring. Deep in my heart, I knew there was more. I longed for a deeper place to grow into in my relationship with Christ and in ministry. I had made one major miscalculation at this point in my life and career. I just assumed I could take all my "stuff" with me. It does not always work that way.

Not really understanding what "done" meant, I quietly challenged myself, "Remember, I have surrendered my will for God's will in my life." I had learned from past experiences to hold everything with an open hand. By this, I simply mean that I had come to recognize God as owner and me as His steward or manager. Because I had chosen to surrender my life into His hands, my life was no longer my own.

Things began to unravel at work. That easy road became hard almost overnight. I began to lose favor at work and at home as the true desires of my heart began coming into the light. Despite a promising and bright career, my heart was turning toward deeper involvement in Kingdom work. I could envision myself giving up my career to serve God in ministry and missions. The tug on my heart created tension between me and my wife as she was now being asked to shift her vision off millionaire status onto the unknown of being the wife of a missionary. She was not interested in being married to a pastor or a missionary. Over the years, I have come to realize the stress this placed on her heart as I asked her to step into my calling. After all, it is common knowledge that many missionaries are poor while some even end up killed or imprisoned.

The only future I could see was a path that followed Jesus straight into the adventure of the unknown. She chose a much different path, one that led us toward divorce as she struggled to head off a future of uncertainty.

Our marriage ended abruptly. It began to feel as if my life had gone airborne and out of control, much like Bodine's truck did at the Daytona Beach 500. Unexpectedly, everything changed in an instant.

Church was no longer my safe haven. I felt it was my duty to speak up when several signs pointed to internal issues that needed to be addressed. Just as I had believed that my wife would welcome my fresh insights and vision, the response of my church family was quite similar. What began with me shedding light on potentially unscriptural practices ended with another divorce of sorts, as I was kicked out of this fellowship for being out of order. It felt as if I was being punished by my wife and my church family for trying to follow God.

My whole-hearted commitment led to the quick demise of my marriage and the destruction of my both my natural and spiritual family.

I barely hung on to hope as three key areas of my day-to-day life fell apart, piece by piece.

Within the short span of only 12 months, everything was gone my marriage, my church family, and my promising career.

For a moment, I felt a bit like Kim in that ball of fire. My whole life exploded, and I felt caught right in the middle of the flames. Eventually, the smoke began to clear. Despite the devastation and the heartbreak, an interesting thing began to occur within my heart. I felt a new sense of freedom emerging out of nowhere as I chose to move into my deepest calling. I stripped off the garments soaked in the past as God began to prepare me for the future. He still had plans for my life. That is the hope I clung to daily as I walked toward His restoration.

I identified in that season with the song entitled My Place in This World by Michael W. Smith. I did not know my place. God began to teach me that there is a vast difference between ministry involvement and a true place of belonging. I had been active in all types of Christian ministry, but I sensed there was still something else on the horizon. I just could never quite put my finger on it.

Only one thing remained familiar after my life exploded. I was still a resident of Orlando, Florida. My friend Debbie introduced me to the owner of a music studio. His name was Greg and he had recorded for some of the biggest names in Rock and Roll such as Deep Purple, Poco, and Foghat just to name a few.

Greg was looking for someone to handle sales and public relations for the studio. I went over to meet him. That is when he asked me a powerful question, "What do you want to do?"

Keep in mind, I have no musical talent whatsoever. I cannot play any instrument. I cannot sing. Nothing. Nada. Zilch.

A quite unexpected answer to Greg's question just jumped out of my mouth. "I want to come and work for you." I even surprised myself. A step had been taken as I began to walk out of my past. I was not running away. I was moving toward God's plan for my future. I was beginning to find my place in this world by finding my perfect place in my Father's Kingdom.

We cut a risky deal that day. No salary, just straight commission on any recording business I could book for the studio. For some crazy reason, despite being broke, I felt like the happiest man alive!

I worked harder than ever with hours that I loved. I would go on the clock around 10:00am and work into the evening, finally winding down around 7:00 or 8:00pm.

Greg was a great boss and is a great human being. A diving accident had altered his world view as he was now positioned to live and lead from a wheelchair. This was not a limited man. For all the years I worked there, I never saw him have a bad day. He made it impossible to hold a pity party for yourself. Looking back now, I am so thankful I was granted that time with him. God used Greg in powerful ways to empower me to not only release my past and move on but to gain the right attitude and perspective along the way.

Weeks turned into months. Despite having the time of my life while working harder than ever, I had not booked a single job. It was embarrassing. The little savings I had was dwindling down to nothing. In the movie Ghostbusters, after starting their Ghostbuster business and not having any customers, Bill Murray says to his buddies as they eat their last meal, "this is the last of the petty cash." I was reminded of that fictional movie scene when I woke up one morning with less than four dollars in my checking account. This was not fiction, but my real life. It was the last of my petty cash.

I had reached the end. From potential millionaire with thousands in the bank and a hefty portfolio of stocks and profit sharing, two houses, and a Harley, I now had barely enough gas to make it to work, but not enough to get home.

I did what any wise executive would do. I blew my last few dollars on a great coffee and drove to work as usual. I still loved what I was doing but, once again, I did not sell anything. With a commission-only contract, I was not entitled to anything. The end of that day rolled around, and it was time to go home. There was only one problem. I was out of gas and out of money.

Just before closing time, Greg wheeled into my office. With no knowledge of my situation, he placed four hundred dollars on my desk and said, "I thought you could use this," and then he wheeled out. It might as well have been the million dollars promised by my earlier career!

I felt rich and free in that moment as I realized that God was at the helm of this new season of my life.

You can't make this up—but Jesus can!

Chapter 19
A WHOLE NEW WORLD

Do not despise these small beginnings.
ZECHARIAH 4:10 (NLT)

I walked into a new industry while my new boss and mentor rolled into my office. Working at Greg's studio opened a whole new world to me. My mind returned to my high school days when many of my friends were talented musicians. Once again, I felt out of place but glad to be here.

If you ever find yourself in the place where you know you were meant for something more than what currently captures your time, do not give up until you find out what it is. Many key Scriptures including Psalm 139 boldly declare that there is a plan for your life. Never give up until you find it. We only get one shot at this life, so we need to make it count!

I began to explore the music business, specifically in Christian music. A God thought entered my brain,

Christian Concerts. What if I was meant to apply all that Greg—and my former jobs—had taught me to promote music that honored God?

I was on a collision course with destiny, as my experience with business came in direct contact with my love for the Lord and music. The point where these intersected led me to another unexpected place—and the outcome was Christian concerts. I began to search for a venue that would allow me to hold my first event.

Any salesman can tell you that this next statement is true. Rejection is always a part of sales. My car sales bootcamp experience would now display its full value. I was a bit naive about how difficult it would be to find a church willing to host a concert targeted for the youth.

Eventually, I got the nod from a Methodist Church only a half-mile from where I lived. At the time of my call, they had just been praying about this same idea. They offered the building with a capacity of over three hundred for free. This was my first break on the path to my new vision.

With the location secured, the search was on for a band. I was still in contact with the youth from my former church in Orlando, so I thought that was a good place to start. I polled the group to get some ideas.

One of the members had spent time at a college in South Florida. While there, she had met a little-known independent band called Tenth Ave North (TAN). This idea came just in time, as their popularity was ready to explode. They would soon sign a record deal, move to Nashville, and go on to receive a Dove Award for Best New Artist.

We hit a home run with this event. Over 250 youth attended. Because TAN was not under a record deal yet, we could legally film the concert. That recording has remained available online for over thirteen years.

A year later, I moved to Nashville, Tennessee. Just as I was pulling into town, TAN came on the radio singing Love Is Here. We were both about to experience a new beginning. Life began again!

You can't make this up—but Jesus can!

Chapter 20
THE DONE DEAL

Behold, I am doing a new thing;
now it springs forth, do you not perceive it?

Isaiah 43:19

I only lived in Nashville for about six months. It was a great time of healing, but I needed to build a strong foundation for my future. While getting my feet wet in the music business, I also realized that I still needed a better paying job.

Much of my spare time was spent sending out resume after resume with no results. I had confined my search to the Nashville area. About to give up, I decided to widen the search to some other states. I struggled with feeling that I might be compromising what God had called me to if I left the Nashville area. But I needed work. I applied for a position with MSC, a company similar to Grainger. To my surprise, I received a call and was plugged into the interview process. About halfway through the process, the interviewing manager said he was transferring to another area and someone else would take over. It turned out to be the same man who hired me at Grainger! I had no idea that he had changed companies because we had not stayed in touch. It was a done deal. I did not even finish the interview. He hired me based on my history with Grainger.

I still wrestled with the thought I might be missing something or giving up on my music dream too soon, but a job in the music business in Nashville was just not happening. I packed my bags, thanked my Nashville hosts, and moved to Asheville, North Carolina.

I was in a new town with a new job and a new sense of purpose. I decided to continue with concert promotion, compelled by a deep desire to bring the Word to people in need of hope. This included a concert series called Sounds of Life.

I connected with a local Care Net Director. They were providing pregnancy counseling services. At the time, Focus on the Family was providing a fifty percent Grant for Ultrasound machines for pregnancy centers. Ultrasounds are extremely effective in changing the minds of women considering abortion. This mission of the concerts was to raise awareness and finances for this important cause.

I did indoor and outdoor concerts. The venue did not matter. Once I booked space with the City of Asheville in a public park. The Director of Parks and Recreation asked me why I wanted this particular park. He told me it was full of drug addicts and homeless people. I said, "Perfect! That's the exact park I want to go to!"

Over time I expanded the artist list beyond Tenth Ave North to include Natalie Grant, Matthew West, Aaron Shust, Laura Story, Todd Agnew, Mark Shultz, and others. I was having the time of my life. It felt like a dream. Mark Shultz really stood out as an amazingly humble and gracious guy, punctuating just how meaningful this season was going to be.

After several years of some difficult and trying times, the Lord was breathing new life and revealing more of His plans for my future. How precious are His promises!

You can't make this up—but Jesus can!

Chapter 21
CAN YOU DUET?

Humble yourselves, therefore, under the mighty hand
of God so that at the proper time he may exalt you.

1 PETER 5:6

If we humble ourselves under the Lord's hand, He
will exalt us in due time. I saw this so clearly when I
left Florida to move to Tennessee. Nashville is the hub
of not only country music, but also Christian music.
I wanted to continue with the concerts and music I
started in Florida while working with Greg at his studio.

Once I arrived in Nashville, I was hosted by friends,
the Carter, and Stanton families. They were like an oa-
sis in the middle of the desert to me.

I found work selling cars. The nice part about this
tour of duty was that the dealership provided a small
salary in addition to commission. Since I had no material needs at the time, I was content with just enough to
live on.

Over the last two chapters, I've shared about bringing Tenth Ave North in to do a benefit concert. Well, let me share another God story that came out of that event.

As I sat discussing the TAN concert idea with the outreach director of Care Net, I told her that all I needed was an opening band for the event. I asked her if she knew anyone who would help us out. She opened her desk drawer and handed me an unopened CD. She told me this young man dropped it off and she never had time to listen to it. Maybe he would be interested. His name was Ryan Larkins.

I listened to the CD and it was amazing, so I reached out to this nineteen-year-old musician. I was starting to realize that I did have music-related talent—the ability to pick out a winner in the crowd.

I pitched the idea to Ryan, along with the purpose of the event and who he would be opening for. He was the worship leader in his dad's church of about thirty people. He was humble and in his down-to-earth style, he agreed to help.

Over the next couple of years, he helped with many events despite the fact I never had enough money in the event budget to pay him. His servant's heart always came through. "I'm just happy to be here."

One day I received a call from Ryan. He said a friend of his was trying out for a new music reality show on Country Music Television (CMT) called Can You Duet. It was a country version of American Idol designed around duet artists. Asked to duet with his friend, he solicited my opinion as he wrestled with turning down the invitation. I encouraged him to go for it.

I thought to myself, "Ryan has it all, the talent, the look, the personality, the whole package. I know it when I see it."

The auditions were swamped, as thousands came to try out. It was a once-in-a-lifetime opportunity. Within a few days, I got the call. Ryan shouted, "I made it!"

Ryan made it but his friend did not make the cut. The show paired him with another individual and it was game on. Each week Ryan would call me as he progressively moved up the ranks. Several times he sent me VIP access to watch the show taping. I remember sitting in the upper level of the club where the show was hosted. One of the judges was up there and I asked who he was. Ryan said that the gentleman was Scott Borchetta, founder of Big Machine Records and Taylor Swift's Manager.

In Revelation 3:8, Scripture promises that God

opens doors no man can close, and He closes doors no man can open. I could see His favor resting on Ryan's life.

Ryan and his duet partner finished third in the show. Naomi Judd, one of the other judges, said that their rendition of the Tennessee Waltz was the best she had ever heard. That video segment is still available to view online.

Ryan seemed more than content with the level at which he finished. I knew that this high-integrity man would never compromise his vision of leading worship and singing for God, despite the pull of secular country music. Ryan remained faithful to his vision and he still writes and performs in Nashville while enjoying a full life with his beautiful wife and three wonderful children.

This season of life served as a powerful reminder for me personally that God promotes people and visions that are wholeheartedly aimed at honoring Him. Ryan, in his humility, also served as a powerful reminder that God will often call us to a different path than the world.

I still look back on those days in wonder and amazement. And I still celebrate Ryan and his success, especially in his decision to honor Jesus and his family above all else.

You can't make this up—but Jesus can!

Chapter 22
LAKEHOUSE LIVE

The voice of the LORD shakes the wilderness.

PSALM 29:8

Asheville brought quite a surprise. Even though I feared that I was giving up a dream by leaving Nashville, the opposite proved to be true. I quickly found the Asheville music scene to be alive and well. More importantly, getting involved proved easier than it had been in Nashville.

This was evidenced by a place called URTV. Charter Cable held a monopoly for cable service in Asheville. In exchange, they agreed to provide three cable channels to local citizens. One of those channels was URTV. Charter provided a full television production studio, with three cameras and all the associated gear. For a mere ninety dollars per year, any citizen could produce their own show on just about any topic and air it to all of Asheville.

This seemed almost too good to be true. Immediately I started reaching out to bands and artists to be guests on a show I called Lakehouse Live. The name of my new show was inspired by the house I lived in when my music career started in Florida at the studio with Greg—that house was on a beautiful lake, and I had never forgotten that new beginning.

I knew nothing about television. The deal came with built-in training, making my ninety-dollar investment almost foolproof. As part of the deal, the station's staff provided lessons to get the producers started.

Every Wednesday at 8:00pm, we had a one-hour slot on live television! We were given thirty short minutes to prep and sound check. The pressure was on as we would be still making adjustments seconds before going live.

It was an amazing experience as I had the opportunity to put everything Greg had taught me back in Florida into this show.

For those who have never had the chance to visit, Asheville is unique—unlike any other town in North Carolina. Many bumper stickers declare "Keep Asheville weird." With something for everyone, this mountain city boasts an urban vibe with a quirky edge as the streets are filled with people from all walks of life. You can encounter a radical new age guru, a self-proclaimed witch, a super-legalistic Christian, and many others on the same block.

On Friday nights in the center of town, there is a drum circle where participants work themselves into a frenzy. Those new age drums can probably be overhead at the Billy Graham training center just a few miles away.

URTV reflected that complexity and diversity. My show was wedged in between fortune tellers and a woman who called herself the "Glo Lady."

During those times, I found myself living in a spiritual battle zone, right on the front lines with all the action, a place I had come to enjoy. I was wrong to think I was missing out by leaving Nashville. I was exactly where I belonged, and those years were just as interesting as the diverse culture I now called home.

You can't make this up–but Jesus can!

Chapter 23
RIGHT CHURCH, WRONG SEAT

And David inquired of the LORD, "Shall I go up?"

2 SAMUEL 5:19

I thoroughly enjoyed promoting concerts as I witnessed God expanding on what He started in Florida and Tennessee. I especially enjoyed meeting the artists and seeing people enjoy themselves.

The whole scene was amazing and spiritually satisfying—or so I thought. I remember an event featuring Natalie Grant held in the Thomas Wolfe Auditorium in Asheville. I was walking down the aisle to an almost packed house. Natalie was singing. Opening acts were Meredith Andrews and Chris Sligh from American Idol. I was out in the crowd observing and thoroughly enjoying this great experience.

There was only one problem and I mean that literally. Every event had at least one major thing go wrong.

I am not saying that I expected these events to go perfectly. The resistance we were encountering was more than that. I had a nagging feeling that something was not right. But how could that be? What could possibly be wrong with promoting Christ through music, doing concerts to raise money and awareness against abortion and other pertinent social issues? Despite wrestling with questions, I could not put my finger on the answer.

Progressively, I was beginning to think the Lord wanted me to drop it all. That feeling would prove to be accurate in due time, but it was yet to be revealed just why. My dream seemed to be unraveling as we encountered weather related cancellation, equipment failure, and rental issues.

At first, I prayed against what was surely enemy resistance, but this proved to be more than spiritual warfare. Sometimes it was hard for me to tell the difference between enemy resistance and the Lord prompting me to a change in direction. This is a key lesson for every Believer who desires to walk in maturity.

This all came to a climax with a Mark Shultz event. It was a fundraiser to raise awareness for a pregnancy center in North Carolina at the Smoky Mountain Center for Performing Arts. It is an amazing venue, featuring high tech and seating for 1,500. What could be better? It was provided for free! We had radio time donated and even free billboard ads. Everything was coming together perfectly.

Advanced ticket sales were slow. I talked myself into believing that many would still show up at the door on the night of the show, but that did not happen. Barely two hundred people showed up as the scenario shaped up to become a financial nightmare. We had agreed to pay the artist over $6,000.00, but we had less than half that amount. During the show as Mark was performing, I was sweating it out. How am I going to go backstage after the show and tell him I don't have enough money to pay his honorarium? My mind would not stop racing as I stressed over the potential outcome.

I spent the showtime praying and repenting. "Lord, even though this makes no sense to me, if you want me to let go of doing concerts I will, but please get me out of this mess. I need to keep my word and I don't want to be embarrassed in the end."

As the show came to a close, I procrastinated. I stood by the exit door and thanked everyone for coming until the whole crowd cleared out. While most dream of a VIP, backstage pass, I dreaded going backstage to face the featured artist. I was living every concert promoter's worst nightmare. Why was this happening?

Before I got to the artist with the bad news, a man I had never met walked up to me. He said, "How much are you out?" In my embarrassment, I found myself thinking, "who are you and what business is it of yours?" He must have recognized the stress in my voice and then calmly he said, "No, no, tell me how much you are out." In humility, I said about 3,500.00. He immediately took out his checkbook and gave me a check for 2,500.00. His daughter who was standing next to him spoke up and said, "I will make up the difference."

What? Was this really happening? The night, and my reputation, were saved at the very last minute!

I thanked those servants as I thanked Jesus for them. They had obeyed the voice of God and that allowed me to walk backstage holding my head high. After taking a few photographs with the artist, I gave Mark the full amount I owed.

It turns out that the man who helped me is the owner and founder of Drake Software, one of the largest tax software companies in the United States and the owner of the performing arts center where that event was held. They still sponsor Christian concerts to this day. I am forever grateful to him and his daughter for stepping up that night as we shared in our passion of bringing the Gospel through music.

It would not be long before God would reveal to me why He wanted me out of the concert business. Once you have confirmed that it is God who is speaking to your heart, obey Him quickly even when it does not seem to make sense.

You can't make this up—but Jesus can!

Chapter 24
JUST FILLING IN

To obey is better than sacrifice.

1 SAMUEL 15:22

When the Lord asks for our obedience, we are indebted to Him whether or not He provides a reason. Many times, He does not give the reason until later. Such was the case when I felt led by God to exit the concert promotion business. God was speaking and I finally got His message at the Mark Schultz event. After I finally obeyed, the Lord brought me backstage, so to speak, to give me the debrief.

The answer became clear as day and was totally in line with His nature as the Lord began speaking. He said, "These artists you have been promoting are already in the public eye. They do not need your help because they are already established. You are doing this because you like working with famous people. I want you to work with the artists no one has ever heard of.

The ones who need your help. These are the ones who are not in the music business and are communicating a pure message that reflects my heart and my will. Go to them and help them." Wow, and ouch. I was amazed and convicted at the same time! I found myself really liking being around music celebrities where I had found a sense of importance in the dynamic of name dropping and celebrity association.

The only thing to do in situations like this is take heed, change direction, and move on. That is how discipleship works. Once again, I found myself moving on.

Many of the concerts I had been promoting featured opening bands, mostly artists who were unsigned and just starting out. They did not typically get paid. The benefits for these artists were product sales, free exposure, and experience. Many of them did not even have CDs since studio time was quite expensive.

Wherever there is a need, there is an opportunity! I decided to open a non-profit recording studio. Once again, my experience working with Greg in Florida was about to pay off. I had already built up a list of clients from having the local television show. The county prepared to shut down URTV because of budget constraints, so this was perfect timing for the next venture. My income was back to normal, so I rented a small building and started with a used laptop computer. It was a small, white MacBook. They said it would not run ProTools, but it worked. It would crash from time to time, but it got me started. You may wonder how I can say with confidence that Holy Spirit knows how to use ProTools and computers. Simple. He taught me. The Bible says, "If any of you lacks wisdom, let him ask God, who gives generously to all without reproach, and it will be given him. But let him ask in faith, with no doubting, for the one who doubts is like a wave of the sea that is driven and tossed by the wind." James 1:5-6 Well, I asked! I am no expert, but I got by until I could find and afford a real technical engineer.

One of my other sayings besides "You can't make this up" is "I'm just filling in until the guy who really knows how to do this shows up."

God fine tuned the ministry to a more precise position. Once an engineer was in place, we started a project with two guys named Steven and Alex. That decision would prove to be a game-changer. I met them in a Christian coffee shop called the Encouraging Cup in Asheville. They were talented but when I first heard them, I thought their style was outdated and I told them so. They were at a low point and thinking about giving up altogether. With music production, you have to be brutally honest to remain on the cutting edge—and I was. Their core talent was amazing. They were living out of state, so the logistics were challenging. I was also still working full time. It took a year of devoting weekends only to this vision, but the project turned out amazing as the musicians were in an extremely creative streak. We had the recording mastered by Richard Dodd who had won a Grammy for his work on Tom Petty's Wildflowers album. As you can see, name dropping has proven to be a hard habit to kick.

With a new band name, Reckless Mercy, and a fresh set of songs on a project called Turning Over Tables, they took it to the churches and anywhere else that would let them play. They toured all throughout the southeast every weekend for almost four years. Thousands were impacted by this album. From conservative Methodists to Biker Churches, the appeal seemed to be universal. Fortunately, many of their music videos can still be viewed online.

Altogether Lakehouse Studios produced roughly a dozen, high-quality albums at no cost for up-and-coming artists. The age of indie productions was in full swing and creativity blossomed. This seemed a perfect way to skirt around the filtering of messages by radio stations and record labels. We were proud to be giving a platform where artists could speak and sing un-censored, as we watched the Gospel message reach thousands.

After five years at MSC, my job ended abruptly, and I was forced to close the studio down. I could have been devastated, but by this time, I had a strong his-tory with the Lord. God was up to something new and I just had to go with the flow.

The wind of His Spirit blows where it will, and I have never been disappointed. Life with God just keeps getting better as His plans unfold.

You can't make this up—but Jesus can!

Chapter 25
THE CHOICE

Go into all the world.

MARK 16:15

When I was released from my job at MSC, I had incredible peace. To many, that would not make sense because I was going from a six-figure annual salary to a mere $1,100.00 per month on unemployment. I was also still paying my wife $1,000.00 per month for support. On paper, that left me with a whopping $100.00 all to myself! Nevertheless, I had an expectation of what would come next and God was giving me a supernatural peace that was overwhelming!

There is a backstory to all this. When I was just seventeen, I had thoughts of ending my life. It was for all the typical reasons: drugs fed my teenage angst and I experienced intense feelings of being all alone in the world. My life came crashing down. I was not a believer, at least not in the typical sense. I remember just not wanting to be here—anywhere had to be better.

I took one last chance that there was a God existing in the universe. I remember saying," if you really do exist, then remove these desires from me and I will dedicate one year of my life to nothing but you." Oh my, wasn't I the generous one? Truly, He deserves it all, but I still had that lesson coming.

Immediately as I spoke those words, I felt something lift. The depression, thoughts of suicide, hopelessness—my mental struggle was gone in an instant. As quickly as the oppression left, I wasted no time forgetting the vow I had just made to God. I was still young, and I had living to do.

Years later, I heard that familiar voice again as He prompted me, "Don't live out the rest your life with an unfulfilled vow to the Lord." Scripture teaches that it is better not to make a vow than to make one and not keep it. From where I was standing, I was glad to do it. After all, if He was calling me to complete what I promised, then surely, He would help me make it through.

It was time to fulfill my vows to my Father. God was about to make a way for me to keep the promise I made when I was seventeen. I had always relied on working to provide for my needs, a place where pride can often enter in.

I was about to experience financial provision in a brand-new way.

A couple of years earlier, I had been introduced to a Methodist Minister named Diane. She had single-handedly secured and started a low power FM Radio Station in Asheville which covered a 20-30-mile radius. It featured Hard Rock/Heavy Metal Christian.

Two weeks after I left MSC, I ran into Diane and asked how the station was doing. Immediately she said, "I'm giving it up and I am supposed to give it to you!" I was shocked and overwhelmed.

True to God's pattern in my life, I knew nothing about operating a radio station! Diane handed over everything, equipment, and all. No money was ever exchanged. There was one catch. The station had operated out of the basement of a Methodist Church and now needed to be moved in thirty days. God will put His children into situations where we are completely dependent upon Him. In fact, I have come to believe that God enjoys walking me through this learning process. One thing was certain, I had learned to find joy at these stages in my journey.

Once again, I drew on Holy Spirit for wisdom. I mean, there was virtually no training and no manual at first on how to operate the software or equipment.

Within the first two weeks of the transfer of owner-ship, a huge revival swept through the streets of Asheville led by an out-of-town group. I was able to broadcast the evening services live. I was having the time of my life!

The radio station also gave the perfect opportunity to play music by the indie artists I had recorded back in the studio before finances forced me to close it down. God was bringing together several pieces of the puzzle and I was enjoying the adventure.

I operated the radio station for a full year while only bringing in a net $100.00 per month from unemployment insurance with no savings and no backup funding. There were a few station donations, but I didn't even have a real paycheck, yet God helped me never miss a single bill or mortgage payment. I'm still in awe of how God provided for me daily. His grace on my bank account left me free to totally focus on the ministry of the radio station, thereby fulfilling the promise I had made at seventeen. This continued for one year before I felt led to search for a new means of employment.

You can't make this up—but Jesus can!

Chapter 26
NO DOWN PAYMENT, NO PROBLEM

And if I go and prepare a place for you, I will come again
and will take you to myself, that where I am you may be also.

JOHN 14:3

At His leading, I took care of God's business while
He took care of my business. I was learning to trust His
guidance and faithfulness at a new level.

While so much was happening on the ministry
front, the desire grew for a home of my own. From the
fiasco of Florida, my credit was destroyed. After a few
years of apartment living, I was getting itchy to settle
down.

When my family had first moved to Florida, we were
not stable enough financially to purchase a home. We
rented a house with an option to buy until we were
able to do so. God brought that season back to my
mind as a possible solution for me now. That arrange-

ment had worked out well, so I thought I would try that approach again.

I looked for the perfect home for a long time. Asheville is in western North Carolina, close to the border of Tennessee. Tennessee is appealing because of the lower cost of living, no state income tax, lower taxes overall, and affordable fuel prices. The border is only thirty minutes from Asheville.

After an exhaustive search, I found a two-story log home just over the border in Tennessee. I was sure it said rental, but I was mistaken. When I called the Real Estate agent, he corrected me. I thanked him for his time and told him that I was looking for a rental with a possible option to purchase. He kept trying to convince me to take a closer look.

I was forced to be upfront. Following a divorce, a foreclosure, and other issues, I was not in the position to buy a home. He persisted, stating that I had nothing to lose. Despite my situation, he insisted that I fill out a credit application. I did it to appease him and settle the whole thing. The reply from the credit union was just what I told him it would be. I did not qualify.

Several days later, I got a call from the CEO of the Credit Union inviting me to come in to talk. "Bottom line, you had a good income with MSC, and I am the CEO of this Credit Union. I can do whatever I want!" The Loan Officer was not in full agreement, as she seemed to look for any reason to kill the deal.

The CEO persisted by asking how much I had to put down. Nothing, I said. Do you have anything for closing costs? Again, I said no. By now I was sensing the Lord was opening the door wide and nothing was going to stop this. Several days later, I received a call I will never forget. Approved, with no money down, no closing costs.

On the day of closing, the loan officer called me. She confessed she had made a mistake. Oh boy, I thought. I started to think this was all too good to be true. She made a mistake alright—in my favor. There were costs belonging to me at closing that she had charged to the credit union by mistake. The net result meant that she could either write me a check or reduce the amount of the loan to account for the $2,000.00 mistake. They were now paying me to buy the house that I could not afford in the first place!

As it turns out, the Real Estate Agent was the CEO's son-in-law. On top of that, this Credit Union was formed in 1947. This home was the only foreclosure in their entire business history. The house had been vacant for a long time and they wanted it off their books. I still live in that house today. My home is a daily reminder that God is good. He goes before us, He anticipates our needs, and He is the keeper of strategies far more majestic than we could ever hope for. The Lord knows how to love and care for His sons and daughters.

You can't make this up—but Jesus can!

Chapter 27
A MAJOR SHIFT

And if anyone will not receive you or listen to your words,
shake off the dust from your feet when you
leave that house or town.

MATTHEW 10:14

For many years, I have balanced traditional employment with significant involvement in outside ministry
efforts. My pastor in Florida modeled this lifestyle of
juggling work and ministry until he retired. I chose to
follow His example. Full time employment has enabled
me to support various ministry efforts over the years
that God has placed in my heart.

I have found that I am not good at fundraising. I
have come to realize that working has allowed me to
avoid donations that could have strings of expectation
or control attached to them.

Going full time in ministry has always been something I aspired to, but I have never been given the

green light. Anytime I would step in that direction, I would hear Holy Spirit say, "not yet."

To go full time, I would need an absolute, no questions asked, clear leading from the Holy Spirit.

One day I finally received the green light.

I had been working as Sales Manager in North Carolina for one of the largest electrical equipment distributors in the world. We had just finished the year and it was the best sales year for my district in the five years I had been there. I felt like it was time to go but I was not going to make the first move.

My manager called me into his office for the annual review. To my surprise, he said, "I am completely dissatisfied with your performance." Furthermore, he added goals and requirements retroactive to my previous year's objectives. My review would show me performing below expectations and there was to be no raise. Wow, I thought, "Well this is definitely my exit message." I had already calculated that if I took early Social Security along with a part time job, my finances would be ok, and I would have more time for ministry. I resigned immediately despite a growing team and a promising career.

As I have learned, God has perfect timing. Within a

couple of days, I received a call from my friend Aarron, a business consultant who helps companies with digital marketing. He told me he had started a landscaping business with a partner who did the work while he did the marketing. The partner left, leaving a growing business with no one to do the work. Not knowing my situation, he asked if I knew anyone interested in partnering with him. I did not have to think very hard to come up with the perfect guy for the open job. We entered into an agreement immediately.

Today, I earn close to my corporate salary doing fifteen to twenty hours of work per week in a job without the stress of those corporate settings. It has truly been a divine exchange that I could never have made happen. The landscaping business also allows me to employ troubled youth who have a hard time finding employment. I am an employer and a mentor, exercising my heart to see sons and daughters take their place in their Kingdom family. With the extra free time, I have been able to travel to the Dominican Republic, Nicaragua, and Pakistan to carry Father's heart for all nations.

When an individual carries a heart for Kingdom ministry, it is important to stay flexible. Multiple times I thought I was in an employment situation for the long haul. For me, it has just been for a season. There is usually a purpose and when the purpose is finished, the door closes and another one opens. It took a long time to figure that out and be comfortable with it.

My advice is don't put God in a box. What He does in your life is a custom fit for you, unique in every way. In John 3:8 the Bible says, "The wind blows where it wishes, and you hear its sound, but you do not know where it comes from or where it goes. So it is with everyone who is born of the Spirit." John 3:8

Just keep your sail up and follow His lead.

You can't make this up—but Jesus can!

Chapter 28
THE FATHER'S LOVE

If a man has a hundred sheep, and one of them has gone
astray, does he not leave the ninety-nine on the mountains
and go in search of the one that went astray?

MATTHEW 18:12

Few things have demonstrated the Father's love quite
like this story. As mentioned earlier, I met a young man
named Christian, but the story begins much earlier.

Back when we took over the radio station, we ended up in a Christian night club in the center of downtown Asheville. It was called Creatures Cafe and was
operated by a couple named Joe and Deb. Their vision
included a music club with no alcohol and Christian
bands to be situated in the heart of the bar scene in
Asheville.

I supplied the bands and moved the radio station
into a cubicle in the front window. WGNW 95.7 The
Choice was now front and center. We would have the

bands play at night and broadcast the music live on the radio station. We also produced a variety of Christian worldview radio shows on topics such as health and wellness, nature, business, and cultural diversity. We aimed to honor Jesus while also highlighting the relevance of Christian faith in daily life. Like the rest of the world, this region deserved to know the truth about the Gospel as a powerful alternative to secular life.

The station was a grassroots effort that empowered more than a dozen people to launch their ministries. Eventually, that season also came to a close but a wealth of great memories remain for those of us blessed by this wave of God's favor.

The memory of one event really stands out. A transgender man who frequented the club came in, as usual, one night. A solo artist was on the stage singing an original song she had written about forgiveness. Halfway through the song, the young man disappeared through a back door that led to the back of the building. That dark and dirty service passageway held the nickname "rat alley" for obvious reasons. It was used for deliveries and trash pick-up. Illicit activities also tended to be attracted to that dark place. That is what prompted me to follow him.

I went back into the alley to make sure there was

no drug use. That is when I found the man sitting on a wooden crate crying and repeating, "I can't do this anymore, I can't do this anymore." He was referring to his transgender lifestyle and the associated pain and disillusionment. With his permission, several of us laid hands on him and prayed fervently as he gave his life to Christ that night.

Later on, after the club closed, I was looking for another building for the radio station and the recording studio. I saw an ad for a commercial building in Mars Hill, NC. There is a Christian College there named after the location in Greece where Paul preached. Before calling the owner, I decided to drive by and scope it out. Mars Hill is fifteen minutes north of Asheville and closer to my house than the original location of the station.

I was disappointed when I pulled up to the front of the building. I thought to myself, "This is not a commercial building." An old movie theatre loomed in front of my eyes. Truth be told, I have a soft spot for old buildings. In fact, that passion extends to almost anything that is run down, past its' glory days, and in need of restoration. That includes people. I believe that is a personality trait I inherited from my Father in Heaven. I am a sucker for broken things and people that the world would label as lost causes.

Curiosity got the best of me and I just had to see inside the dilapidated theatre. My ministry partner Shelley was with me. Shelley had been my right hand in many of these crazy adventures. I could not do it all otherwise.

We went around to a side door and found it unlocked! We had to jump up into the doorway because the steps were missing. It was dark inside but there was still enough light to see the basic structure.

It was like walking back in time. Tattered red velvet curtains hung from the ceiling. Torn seats and a small wooden stage with rotten holes completed the tour. The roof had multiple holes and the previous day's rain was still dripping in. This building was an inch away from being a total loss. It felt a bit as if it could cave in on our heads at any moment.

I looked at Shelley. The smirk on her face said, "I am up for it. Are you?"

Long story short, I entered into a lease-purchase agreement and brought my dusty tools out of storage. That is a book in itself, but I will stay on track with this story.

Two years and thousands of dollars later, The Mars Hill Radio Theatre was re-opened. Family movies,

Christian concerts, and special events were held in the 1947 single-screen theatre. We operated for another two years. I could devote several chapters to the stories that emerged from the rubble and rebuilding of the theatre. People said it was a foolish venture, but they said that about Nehemiah too as he tackled a massive rebuilding project long ago.

At the end of four years, I was ready to complete the purchase. The original purchase price was $130,000.00 but now with the improvements, the value escalated upwards of $250,000.00. I was approved with no money down due to the sweat equity in the building. While improvements and modifications would be ongoing, it was fully operational, and the retro vibe was amazing.

Then, a week before closing, the Lord said, "Don't buy it." That's right, "Don't buy it!"

If I had not learned the hard way from many previous experiences, I might have argued, procrastinated, or outright rebelled. But having learned a lesson or two from the past, I simply said, "Yes. Jesus, you are my Lord." One of the hardest prayers you will ever pray is when you say, "Not my will but Yours will be done." Since Jesus had prayed that prayer when His life hung in the balance shortly before His crucifixion, I counted it an honor to be able to yield my desires in this situation to His perfect plan.

When I choose to obey God in radical

ways, I have stopped expecting others to understand. Sometimes, I don't understand myself, but I find the Lord's leading to be perfect in every way.

In the middle of a revival in Jerusalem, Holy Spirit instructed Phillip to go out into the desert. That is where he preached the Word to the Ethiopian who brought the Gospel back to his home country. You can read the amazing account in Acts 8:26. Most people don't expect to find much in the desert, but men and women who follow God have learned that living water can even flow from those dry places with just one touch from God.

Shelley was on board before the words left my mouth. Most everyone else thought I was crazy. The confusion of others was compounded by the fact that the Lord did not give me a reason. I was ok with that because, in my mind, He did not owe me a reason. I was going to follow His voice whether He gave a clear rational or not. He was in the lead, not me.

If He is Lord, just do what He tells you. That is hard for many Christians to do. For me, looking back, anytime I was tempted to resist His leading, I allowed my head to get in the way of my heart. Some of you may be able to relate. This reminds me of a command found in Proverbs. "Trust in the Lord with all your heart, and do not lean on your own understanding. In all your ways acknowledge him, and he will make straight your paths. Proverbs 3:5-6.

Many principles of the kingdom will seem foolish to the human mind because the natural mind seeks to fulfill the desires of our flesh, while our spirit seeks after the things of God's Kingdom as we come into maturity.

In my deal with the owner, if I decided to vacate the lease without buying, all the improvements I had done were to remain with the building at no obligation to him. I walked away from it all with nothing owed to me. He inherited all the improvements and the value of my sweat equity. Four years of hard work, thousands of hours, and countless dollars. All gone in one act of obedience.

The owner of the building was shocked. He now had a highly desirable piece of property for sale, and it sold quickly.

Like an army private awaiting orders from the captain, I went into "what now?" mode. It was not an attitude or feeling like I was owed an explanation. It was more of an expectancy. I pondered what the Lord had up His sleeve. I felt this shift in purpose as I waited for the reason to emerge. The next step revealed itself in a matter of two weeks.

The next building, where we still meet today, is called the Red Rhino. It used to be a teen club but now it's used for Bible study and church services. This building was made available at no charge thanks to my friend Ted who holds the rights to this building. We went from paying $1,000.00 per month for rent to now only covering the cost of utilities.

One night, after walking away from the theatre, my friend Ted who has worked with youth for over thirty-five years brought two teens to the gathering. One of those teens was Christian who was seventeen at the time. He shared his story which included the conditions under which he grew up. I feel honored that Christian has chosen to feature his testimony in this book because it is a glorious picture of how God can lift any person out of unthinkable hardship.

Childhood experiences can make or break an individual. I praise God that nothing is impossible for any person when God is invited into the story.

The night Christian first came to the Red Rhino, he was on an evening pass from the children's home where Ted worked and where DB was on lockdown. At some point in the service, I prayed and delivered a Word from the Lord that DB was destined for great things. God sees us in our future and according to what He has purposed. Often those words prove to be worlds away from our current situations.

After that word was released, something changed. The Bible says in multiple places that Jesus was moved with compassion. We do not operate mechanically as servants executing our Master's will. God's plan is for His ambassadors to carry love and compassion in our daily life, including all types of faith gatherings. He is far more concerned with our heart and motivation than our ability to pull off a perfect church service or event. If His spirit is in me then His compassion is inside of me, motivating me in the direction He wants to go as I submit to Him.

From that moment it became clear why the theatre had to go. For one, Christian would probably never have visited the original location. God had brought him here to the center of downtown. The still small voice of the Lord began to whisper, "Christian is my precious son. Take care of him."

Wow! The Lord was inviting me into a place far more important than any job or ministry start-up. He was entrusting me with the life of His son.

While man looks at the outer person, God looks at the heart. God saw this young man as precious. All the behaviors that the world took offense at were superficial and even insignificant in the eyes of his Father, regardless of how serious they were. Please do not misunderstand me. We do account for our sinful mistakes, but God sees us covered in the blood of His son. He envisions our highest identity and He communicates with us and calls us accordingly.

Little did I know that through this upcoming experience I was about to learn more about the Father's love than any book could teach me. The theatre had to go because God wanted unhindered access as my full attention was about to be directed to one person for a time. As I pondered about how far God is willing to go for a single person, He prompted me to consider the value of a single life. He looked ahead to the financial and time resources which would be required for me to participate in all He had planned. He said in a voice as close to audible as I had ever heard, "This is my son, watch over him."

In a general sense, I know we are always supposed

to watch over others, but this was different. The emphasis was strong, like a direct order given by a commanding officer. God was inviting me into the meaning of the parable of the lost sheep. That story is not as much about the sheep as it is about the shepherds. How far they were willing to go for the one.

The question asked of those ancient shepherds now falls on me in a fresh way. How far was I willing to go for one? We live in a culture in which one might do exceptional things for a family member but that is not often the case for a stranger. The Scripture that says, while I was still a sinner Christ died for me, came alive! Was I willing to do the same for one who God was calling a precious son? My level of maturity was now being tested at a new level. It felt as if my answer to God in this situation carried a weight I had not experienced in prior ministry situations.

You can read the story in Matthew 18 and Luke 15. If you look closely you will see that Jesus confronts the crowd with a strong statement when He suggests that if a man loses one sheep out of a hundred, that shepherd would go after the lost one. Then He says, "What do you think?"

At that moment, Jesus was inviting that crowd of listeners and every future reader to come to honestly assess our priorities. In a straight-forward manner, He wants to know if you and I will leave the ninety-nine for the one who is lost.

Sometimes, I still tend to think with the mind of a businessman. It would be professionally foolish to walk away from ninety-nine good, stable employees to risk going after one, rebellious wild card. While many human leaders forsake the straggler in pursuit of stability and economic gain, I am sure thankful to have a Father who does not think the way I do. God, our Creator, is not motivated by the same things that drive the average person. God is love and that beautiful character attribute does not make room for Him to leave a single individual behind. His sole motivation is love and that motivation is often at odds with our desire for money, security, and the absence of fear. God is not willing that any should perish. As 2 Peter 3:9 assures us, "The Lord is not slow to fulfill his promise as some count slowness, but is patient toward you, not wishing that any should perish, but that all should reach repentance."

I long to grow into a heart like that.

In the story, Jesus says "and if he finds it." He is cautioning upfront that there is no guarantee of success even if you do this for the one. It is an act of faith.

Jesus died for many. As the good Shepherd, He laid down His life for us (the sheep are an illustration of people) but not all receive. It is a choice to accept Him or not. Knowing there was no guarantee that we would follow, God sacrificed it all on our behalf anyway! That illustrates your value to the Father.

I started visiting Christian at the home where he was enrolled in a mandatory program. I would occasionally come bearing lunch or dinner. Like any teen, he preferred fast food over the food they provided, and he had a favorite—chicken quesadillas.

I am sure he wondered much about me and my motivation. He may have even thought I was weird or opportunistic about his situation. Troubled individuals have often encountered and come to expect the worst of themselves and others. The world often has a catch when seeming to play nice. This situation prompted his skepticism. The way of the world is often to give while expecting something in return. Christian was about to encounter a very different individual, and I am not referring to myself here; I am referencing Jesus.

Jesus is remarkably unique. He has no catch, no hook. He loves because He IS love. It is His nature and His character that are promised to never change.

When you love people who have been hurt, you can expect their guard to be up waiting for the hook. Even salvation can be a hook if offered in the wrong way. We do not share

the Gospel so we can score points or take possession of God's sons and daughters! We must share the Gospel because of His compassion that lives in us. God brings us to maturity so we can invest our journey in the lives of those in need of our loving acceptance and wisdom.

One day during a visit, Christian told me he still had several weeks to go before completing this required program. I spontaneously replied, "You will get out early." I hoped I had not given him false hope, as I truly sensed God's favor on his remaining days in that place.

I humbly prayed asking God to back me up. He certainly did. There was a group meeting later that afternoon with the caseworker and probation officer. Just as I had sensed, Christian was released early. This would prove to be the first of many Divine interventions on his behalf. When he was released, I recruited him to work in my landscaping business. I told him that if he was interested, I could already envision turning the business over to him someday.

I was getting to know his strengths, which included intelligence, a sharp mechanical aptitude, and a remarkable ability to hold a conversation with total strangers effortlessly.

Eventually, I invited Christian to be my roommate. I saw it as a way to make work logistics less complicated and a way to mentor him in daily life. He took a room upstairs in my house. He took driver's education, got his license, and his first car. Moving into adulthood is difficult, even under the best of circumstances. Making choices, dealing with the results of those choices—both good and bad—create this roller-coaster of ups and downs for young adults. The older generation needs to keep that in mind to gain the ability to bear with younger adults and youth who are navigating their way to independence.

While early in the process of writing this book, I took a break to spend an hour and a half with Christian going through various Scriptures. God is already speaking to him through dreams and circumstances and I have a deep desire to see him be able to discern God's voice and direction. That is what many of our days together look like in between digging and planting in the natural. God is uprooting past wounds and planting fresh anointing.

Three months later, Christian is on fire for God. When the Spirit of God enters a person, everything changes. Not only has Christian changed, but I have faith that he is becoming a world changer. I believe that he is destined to impact everyone he encounters. While I fully expect Christian to write his own book someday, I am truly honored that he has chosen to share part of his testimony as a featured bonus of this book.

Jesus often referred to Himself as the Good Shepherd who laid down His life for the sheep.

The Lord longs for us to walk in His ways and to invest in others. What are you willing to lay down? Is it a career, material things, your identity or reputation, your sense of success? The Father gave what was most precious to Him, His Son. Jesus gave His life. These last two years have demonstrated to me the depth of the love of the Father as I have never seen before and I am forever changed. I have gained a glimpse into the Father heart of God by sharing life and home with a young man in a way that would not have been possible if we only encountered each other at an event or church.

You can't make this up—but Jesus can!

Chapter 29

GOD'S MOUNTAIN

I look up to the mountains.

Psalm 121:1 (NLT)

I live thirty minutes north of Asheville, NC in a little spot called Flag Pond, Tennessee where the only commercial enterprise is a part-time post office. My home is an old, two-story log cabin. I love the peaceful setting complete with a running stream in the front yard and a small pond out back. Since it is high up in the mountains, no air conditioning is even required. I open the windows in late April and close them in October. The Lord knew exactly what he was doing when He placed me here in this tranquil setting.

My oldest son lives close by in Asheville. I have another son in Orlando and two daughters up North. Since I still have my pilot's license, I thought purchasing a plane would make visiting them easier. I heard there was an abandoned airstrip near my house in an area called Wolf Laurel. It was designed as a high-end residential area but in the economic downturn of 2008, home sales plummeted, and the project stalled.

One day after scouting out the abandoned strip, a friend took me up to the mountaintop that sits high above the airstrip. Immediately after cresting the top of the mountain on four-wheelers, the words "God's Mountain" jumped into my head. It was like the opening scene from the Sound of Music where Julie Andrews is twirling and singing, "The Hills are Alive!"

I was overwhelmed with the beauty as I scanned the almost 360-degree view of the mountains as far as the eye could see and a plateau field that is just breath-taking. I thought to myself, "Someday I will build a chapel here." My friend who is well off financially said, "I tried to buy this piece of land but could never afford it."

Reluctant to leave the serenity and beauty of this place, we climbed aboard the four-wheelers and headed back down the mountain.

The next day I spoke with another friend who had some business interests nearby. I told Rick how impressed I was with the view. He informed me that a one-acre portion there was now owned by the county as it was taken back for unpaid taxes. He went on to inform me of how this county has a process in place for the purchase of land they own. From county records, it looked like it once sold for $300,000.00, a price tag well beyond my means at that time. Just out of curiosity I asked Rick, "What do you think a person would have to offer in submitting a bid?" He suggested that I try offering $2,500.00. I could not believe what I was hearing. My friend believed it possible for me to purchase that acre for pennies to the dollar of its true value of nearly $300,000.00. He assured me that was a real possibility. I followed his lead, prepared the bid, and submitted it.

When God makes a way for something, the gates of hell will not prevail against it. People feel the spirit of God and His presence and purpose in a special way on this mountain. This would not be the sort of gift for making a profit. There is a special purpose for this place that is yet to be revealed.

After several days I was astonished that the bid was accepted! The definition of stewardship is to care for something like it's yours when you don't own it. I did not gain access to this land for my own profit. I saw this mountain top as a place of worship and perhaps even a place to build a chapel for all to enjoy. I believe that is why He entrusted it to me. It will serve a great Kingdom purpose in His perfect timing.

I currently rent the land to campers. This allows me to share the natural beauty of the place while generating income for the ministry. There is a huge wooden cross placed up there and it has been used for several weddings. Even non-believers marvel at the peace they feel sleeping under the stars or sitting by an open campfire.

You can't make this up—but Jesus can!

Chapter 30
GET OUT THE MANUAL

Are not two sparrows sold for a penny? And not one of them will fall to the ground apart from your Father.

Matthew 10:29

October 6, 2017, was an unusual day. Just three days after my birthday, I woke up as usual with one major, startling exception. As I swung my legs off the bed and my feet hit the floor, I felt an unusual numbness. It was like when a limb falls asleep with pins and needles, only more intense.

I stood up thinking the feeling would come back to my leg and foot once blood began circulating again by moving around. I reasoned that I had probably laid wrong on that side of my body. I headed to the shower and tried to shake it off. I began to realize there was something wrong as the problem became worse instead of better as it spread to include my arm as well as my leg.

I don't know if this is exclusively a male trait, but I am the master of denial. I thank God that I have never had any serious injury, disease, or sickness. I had only been in the hospital once for a broken hand and certainly never overnight.

I kept trying to shake this off as I dressed and headed off to work. About halfway there, the symptoms intensified. I was having an increasing amount of trouble controlling the gas and brake pedal. About that time, I heard the Lord whisper, "You are having a stroke. Pull into the market and get some aspirin." Fear tried to sink its sharp ugly thoughts into my mind. I could not believe this was happening to me.

I limped up to the automatic front doors of the market. There on the ground, just at the spot where the doors opened, was a dead sparrow. It was not mangled. It had no visible sign of injury. In fact, I thought it was sleeping. I did not know it was dead until I brushed it with my foot. I gently whispered to the Lord, "Is this the time you are going to take me home? If so, I may be a little nervous, but I am ok with that." What came back to me was the Scripture that not a sparrow falls to the ground that our Father does not know about.

At that moment, I knew it was going to be a rough

day, but faith entered my spirit with an assurance that everything was eventually going to be ok. I headed over to the blood pressure machine near the prescription counter. My pressure was so high the machine could not register it. I bought a bottle of generic aspirin and swallowed three. Then I jumped back in my car and headed to work.

I can hear you calling me stupid. Here was part of my reasoning. I live in the middle of the country and I thought my chances were better heading into town than waiting for an ambulance. By the time I got to work, the stroke was getting into high gear. My office was on the second floor and I only made it up half-way before I collapsed. One of the guys helped me to my desk where I proudly proclaimed, "Jack, I'll be ok if I just rest here a few minutes." The branch manager, Dwayne, insisted on talking me to the Emergency Room in his truck.

That experience was as you might expect. Doctors and nurses rushed into high gear, administering tests while starting an IV through which I could be given any needed medicine. It took all day for experts to confirm what the Lord had spoken to me back in the parking lot earlier that morning. I had experienced a stroke.

At this point, I had been in the Emergency Room

all day, now unable to walk or stand. I was already quite uncomfortable with my first real visit to a hospital. Fortunately, my facial muscles and speech were not affected, but I had minimal voluntary control over my arm or leg.

While an inpatient room was being prepared for my admission to the hospital, I knew that I needed God to prepare my heart. I did not know what the future held. Even though I could not stand on my own, I leaned hard into my God-given faith. I had to believe that it would all turn out ok. Faith comes from hearing. I heard the voice of the Lord say, "In Him do I place my trust!"

To be blunt, after being in there most all day for testing and admission, my bladder was full. Not being used to hospital confinement, I wanted to use the bathroom by myself, but the nurse would not allow any of that. She handed me the plastic bottle. When she did, an unusual thought passed through my mind. I had full function of my left side but not of my right, so what happens to my body parts in the middle? I had no experience in these matters, but I was about to find out. Would everything be normal? Would I be incontinent? So are the countless functions we daily take for granted.

I used the plastic bottle and embarrassingly handed

it off to the nurse. Everything seemed normal but when I handed it off to the nurse, I looked down only to notice that the bed was soaked. I had wet the bed and did not even know it.

My heart dropped and fear gripped me at a more intense level as I was realizing what I thought was my worst nightmare. My fear was interrupted as the nurse yelled out loudly as if a mouse had just crawled across the floor. As I moved my stare from the bed to that nurse, I saw her make a beeline for the bathroom—all while holding a leaking plastic bottle! There was a defect in the bottle, a hole in the bottom that had leaked on the bed and was now leaking on the floor! Wow, what a scare! Perhaps I was going to be ok after all. I went from petrified to full of faith faster than you could imagine. From that point, I chose to believe that I was going to return to 100% normal in every way despite the road ahead of me.

I spent a few days in the hospital where a barrage of tests revealed a normal heart, no blockages, or other issues. The culprit identified was high blood pressure.

My prayer shifted this way. If the Lord wasn't taking me home, then I wanted everything restored fully. I am convinced that God does not put sickness on people. It is the devil who comes to steal, kill, and destroy. Jesus came that we would have life and life abundantly. This concept is made clear in John 10:10: "The thief comes only to steal and kill and destroy. I came that they may have life and have it abundantly."

This was an attack. The Bible clearly teaches that no weapon formed against you will prosper. It does not say that weapons will never be formed. Only that they will never prosper. The side effects of this stroke had to go! I stood on promises found in the Word of God.

Once I was released from the hospital, it was off to rehabilitation where I would regain function. The brain is a complicated organ. Its construction could never happen by evolution. In my case, I pictured all the pathways where information travels to the body from this central control station known as the central nervous system. I imagined how a landslide or avalanche can block a highway, leading travelers forced to find a detour. It is known in medical science that the brain has an amazing ability to find new routes and pathways to get signals and messages out to the organs and limbs that are initially blocked by events such as a stroke. I was now desperately hoping that my brain would quickly find a detour that would allow it to communicate with my right arm and leg.

I soaked my mind in Scripture and watched countless videos on divine healing. I surrounded myself with faith-filled brothers and sisters. When I wasn't watching or reading, I bathed myself in worship music. The years have taught me that this is my best battle strategy.

This situation forced me to take some basic medications that I am really against except in extreme cases. One night I was overwhelmed with anxiety, depression, and anger. I was ready to bite everyone's head off! It turns out that the doctor gave me a Prozac without my consent with the excuse that they were testing to see if it helped stroke patients recover faster. Equating my extreme emotions with this surprise medication, I told him never again. I saw that I was going to have to become more proactive in my own recovery. From that point on, I monitored every medication.

With lots of time on my hands, I soaked myself in all the teaching videos I could find on divine healing. I also blocked any input, medical and non-medical that would hinder my recovery. I informed only a select few who would stand with me in faith. Years ago, I had read about John G. Lake and his healing ministry. I read about how he trained divine healing technicians and ministered healing to thousands spanning from Africa to Spokane, Washington. Much of his work and sermons can be found online alongside people like Katherine Kuhlman, Smith Wigglesworth, and other legendary Christians who ministered healing.

My current situation gave me the motivation and the time to study out answers to some questions on healing that had been lingering for years. I mused:

Why do some get healed and some not?

Is a healing ministry only for some and not all?

Does God still really raise the dead?

I just had to know! Shelley, my ministry partner, found out that Lake's ministry was still thriving. This led me to discover Curry Blake. The testimony of how he inherited the Lake ministry is profound. I learned that Lake's teachings were still available from Curry, along with added concepts from Curry's experience and study. Lake promoted the truth that any believer is capable of ministering healing and that it is not reserved for a select few. He trained many using a manual called the Divine Healing Technician Manual (DHT) which Curry has continued to use as a cornerstone of his ministry.

Along with my ministry team, I attended a live training session in January of 2020, and it revolutionized our outreach philosophy and approach. During my days in rehabilitation, I took advantage of having time to soak in the online teaching that was available from Curry.

We have a promise in Scripture. In shows in Deuteronomy 4:29, Proverbs 8:17, Jeremiah 29:13, Matthew 7:7, Luke 11:9, and Acts 17:24.

God is faithful to His promises. When we seek Him with our whole heart, we will find Him. I was seeking and God was revealing truth.

My recovery became super-charged as I took this spiritual teaching as seriously as I took my physical rehabilitation. Every day, my body showed a vast improvement over the previous day. The staff and physical therapy team were amazed at how fast motor function was returning. I had a routine of switching back and forth between watching videos and therapy workouts.

Rehab was a great place to witness. After about a week, I acquired a roommate. He was a severe alcoholic and the staff knew I was a Christian. I believe they thought it would help and they were right. I'll call him Ernest for his privacy because he could have been a twin to Ernest Hemmingway, beard, and all.

One day the nurse brought him some clothes because he had minimal personal belongings. I turned to see him wearing a Key West shirt. God has a sense of humor that I have come to appreciate.

One day my friend Rick was visiting. We were just sharing our experiences with God. The curtain was drawn between Earnest's bed and mine. Suddenly, Earnest pulled back the curtain and said, "Would you guys pray for me?" We did and he thanked us.

The next day, I heard Earnest half talking to himself loud enough for me to be able to easily hear. Ernest verbally recalled in disbelief much of how he had spent his recent months. He reminded himself how he used to sit in his recliner night after night. He would get out his loaded, forty-five caliber pistol. He would then pro-ceed to pull back the hammer, stopping each night just before pulling the trigger on his own life.

He went on to exclaim to himself—and to God—how all those oppressive thoughts were now gone and how grateful he was to the Lord for delivering him. He thanked the Lord out loud for the power found only in the name of Jesus.

Much like Ernest, I found myself thanking God as well. In record time, all my motor abilities returned. My recovery was unprecedented according to my physical therapists. Soon thereafter, with all my rehab goals successfully fulfilled, the therapists ran out of things for me to do. Although still a bit weak and shaky, it was finally time to go home. I felt as if the stroke had never happened.

I remember the day I took a leap of faith and started to run. Amusing myself as I tested the limits of my recovery in much the same way a small child perfects motor skills by learning to run and play. I felt like Forest Gump when he is being chased and his leg braces come flying off! Freedom!

In a recent conversation with a physician who visited our church, I shared my recovery story. God never needs us to stretch the truth about what He has done, and for that reason, I am careful to never exaggerate. Some people recover from strokes and some are not nearly as fortunate. Doctors remain amazed that I have no residual effects whatsoever. Since this horrifying experience, I have yet to meet another stroke survivor who recovered one hundred percent. This makes me realize how truly blessed I was through this ordeal. My gratitude to God fuels my compassion when given the opportunity to pray for and minister to other stroke survivors.

You can't make this up—but Jesus can!

Chapter 31
BREAKING THE RESISTANCE

I have given you authority ... over all the power of the enemy.

LUKE 10:19

On my first trip to Pakistan, I had absolutely no idea what to expect. Pakistan is the third most harshly persecuted country in the world as it pertains to those of the Christian faith. It's a harsh environment where Believers make up approximately 1.3% of the total population.

My friend Kathy is the founder of Reflections of Hope (ROH) Ministries. She lives in the United States with her husband, Tahir, a native of Pakistan. ROH is a support organization serving churches near Lahore, Pakistan. One of their main missions is to dig wells and install hand pumps to supply clean, fresh water to the surrounding villages.

While I was there, I witnessed the water shortage and became aware of the vast need for this outreach. Our team stayed in a town called Renala Kurd. Near the end of our trip, we held a conference to equip and encourage pastors, their families, and congregations. Approximately five hundred attended.

After a time of worship and a powerful Gospel message, we held a time of personal prayer ministry. A man was brought to me by a friend of his and I was abruptly told that he was possessed by a demon. The friend longed to see this man be free from all oppression and he was trusting me to take action.

The man was not coherent and was clearly being tormented. On the surface, it appeared much like he had a mental or psychological condition as his eyes rolled back in his head. He seemed completely disconnected from the world around him as he required physical assistance to hold him upright.

As I began to pray in the name of Jesus, he began to growl. It was as if the name of Jesus was pushing a button attached to a speaker that only released the unintelligible utterance. I began to command every demonic spirit and all forms of oppression to go according to the promise of authority in Scripture, which allows true followers of Jesus Christ to do so. "And these signs will accompany those who believe: in my name they will cast out demons; they will speak in new tongues; they will pick up serpents with their hands; and if they drink any deadly poison, it will not hurt them; they will lay their hands on the sick, and they will recover." Mark 16:17

The next fifteen to twenty minutes felt like an eternity. The demon was not budging. Feeling as if I had hit a spiritual brick wall, I asked the Lord for wisdom to meet the challenge before me. Jesus whispered for me to do to the demon what the demons do to God's people. I asked the Lord to clarify what He meant. Holy Spirit then instructed me and gave me permission to torment the demon. I want to be clear here that Jesus would never ask a leader to torment a human being. The torment was to be targeted to the oppressive demonic forces that were holding this man in bondage.

In an instant, I understood what would be most tormenting to a demon. The thought came like a flash. Tell the devil's sent one about the beauty of Jesus, the blood of Jesus, and the Kingship of Jesus. Then tell them about their destiny. Talk about the love of Jesus.

I began to speak out loud as I extolled every virtue of Jesus that Holy Spirit brought to my heart and mind. Instantly, I envisioned fingernails scratching across a chalkboard, driving the demon up a wall as I went on about the love and beauty of Jesus. I declared to the Heavens that I was willing to stay there all night on divine assignment to evict this trespassing tormentor. I was determined not to budge. Then all at once, the demon departed. It was like an electrical switch was turned off. The man's eyes opened, and I was finally able to converse coherently with the man through the interpreter.

I asked if he wanted to receive Jesus. To my surprise, he said no. I was amazed but then I realized what he had just been through and how his culture had not taught him about the wonders of a life in Christ. He deserved to know more so he could make an informed decision.

I explained how God's Word teaches that demons will attempt to return much the same way that a squatter seeks to inhabit an abandoned building (Matthew 12:45). His solution to lasting freedom was only one simple decision away. No demon wants anything to do with a human spirit full of Jesus.

I felt deep compassion for this man wash over me as I plead with him to understand how much Jesus loved him and longed to set him free into a life in Christ through salvation. It broke my heart to envision that demonic force returning with hordes of evil companions seeking to rob his new-found freedom. The Lord brought revelation and understanding to the man who stood before me and he embraced Jesus as Savior in a moment of victory.

You can't make this up—but Jesus can!

Chapter 32
HIGH ALTITUDE HEALING

They who wait for the LORD shall renew their strength;
they shall mount up with wings like eagles.

Isaiah 40:31

After an incredible mission trip to the Dominican Republic last year, I boarded the four-hour flight home to North Carolina along with my ministry partners and friends, Heath, Mike, and Tim.

As I settled into my seat, I was still thinking about one of the last miracles which took place the day before we left. We were walking along the street and came upon a vendor selling barbecue chicken. The woman attending the grill had a brace on her leg. After starting up a casual conversation, we learned she contracted polio at age five. I would assume her current age was about forty.

We asked if we could pray for her. At first, she looked puzzled but then gladly accepted the invitation.

As she sat in a chair, Tim raised her legs gently and began to pray. The leg which had been affected by polio was noticeably shorter by about an inch and a half.

As the prayer began, a crowd started to assemble. Intuitively, I hit the record button on my phone to capture the unfolding moment on video. Once there was a full crowd, the leg began to shift into alignment and lengthen. It was as if God was waiting on the witnesses to get in position.

Ironically, the onlookers included a group of doctors traveling on vacation. The expression on their faces was priceless. When intellectuals and science-minded people encounter miracles that defy everything they have been taught, it confronts and insults human logic. The foundations in their mind were visibly shaken. Once they saw the leg straighten out, many of the onlookers came forward in pursuit of personal healing. One doctor had deafness in one ear, and another suffered from shoulder pain.

In the moments that followed, many other kinds of healings took place among these doctors! We marveled that from this point on, wherever they went in their medical practices, this was a day they would never forget. I prayed God would always remind them that education and skill can only take you so far. The rest is dependent upon God showing up to partner with our limited human efforts. Doctors can diagnose, but only God can heal.

Now back to the flight. I was sitting in the middle seat, the one every traveler dread being assigned to. No elbow room left me feeling confined. Heath was seated to my right while the aisle seat was occupied by a woman from Korea. She told me how she had been in the Dominican as part of a team of doctors who had come to outfit locals with prescription eyeglasses. She noticed me as I sat there reviewing the recording of the woman's leg growing out. I offered to show her the video.

First, she said that she had never experienced a miracle. Next, she told me about an auto accident she had survived approximately one year ago. In the crash, there was damage to her leg and shoulder. Her leg injuries required surgery which had not been successful. This caused her to refrain from having the needed surgery on her shoulder.

After she finished watching the video, I suggested prayer for her shoulder. It was not long or drawn out, just simply, "In the name of Jesus, be healed!" Before the prayer, she could not lift her arm above horizontal and she was in constant pain. After prayer, she quickly reported that all pain was gone as she lifted her arm straight up into the air, testing the parameters of her miracle! God had evicted her pain just as surely as He had evicted that demon earlier.

Immediately, she started crying and shouting. "It's gone. It's gone. The pain is gone!" Hearing the commotion, the flight attendant came down the aisle to investigate. The flight attendant tried to ask some questions but could not get through all the crying and blubbering. Finally, I told the attendant that it was all ok. The woman kept her arm up for another thirty minutes. After a while, I suggested that she could lower her arm. She vehemently said, "No. I want everyone to know what Jesus did for me!"

God had been with us on the ground in the Dominican Republic. Now, He was still with us at 35,000 feet in the air.

You can't make this up—but Jesus can!

Chapter 33
YOU HAVE MAIL

Your word is a lamp to my feet and a light to my path.

PSALM 119:105

As I pondered what story to use to close out this book, it was handed to me from Heaven.

I did not feel that I needed another confirmation for writing this book, but it seems that Holy Spirit wanted to eliminate every possible doubt by miraculously financing its production.

If you read the earlier chapters, then you already know my life has had a range of financial ups and downs. The Apostle Paul said he had learned how to be content both in times of plenty and in times of lack. I don't know if I could say I have always been content, but I can say He has never forsaken me.

During one significant period of loss when the Florida season of life was coming to a close, I used my

401K just to get by. With that hard decision came the usual IRS penalties in the form of interest and taxes. As a result, any tax refunds which had been due to me for the last twelve years have all bypassed my bank account, returning straight to the IRS. I have gotten so used to the consequences of that season of financial instability that I don't think much of it anymore. Tax time comes and I dutifully sign off to release any refund dollars to pay toward the debt that accumulated.

In 2018, I filed an extension so that I had until October to complete the tax return. Several months after filing that return, it was returned because I had forgotten to sign it. I promptly signed and returned to be in full compliance with my new deadline.

As I was wrapping up the writing phase for this book, the calendar marked February of 2020. Here, nearly two years later, I had never heard anything regarding that 2018 tax return despite having always received a letter officially earmarking my return dollars as another year's payment toward that debt. I forgot about it over time after making a mental note that I had to be getting close to having the debt paid off.

Meanwhile, as my writing concluded, the Lord provided the team to assist me in getting my book into print. I traveled to North Carolina from my Tennessee home to meet with Kim, the team leader, and discuss what it would take to complete my vision. While I had completed much of the initial writing, my manuscript was now ready for wordsmithing, editing, and design—all the pre-print pieces of the puzzle.

Kim agreed to reduce my cost significantly from standard rates because her team has a passion for helping to release Kingdom-building books. This process is a costly one because of the skill and detail work involved, so even with generous discounts, I still needed the Lord to provide several thousand dollars for this book to get out of my heart and onto paper. This was not too hard for God.

I learned along the way that when the Lord prompts me into action, He wants me to focus on His face and the vision instead of on my checkbook or bank account. If God calls you to step out, do so in faith. Don't be delayed by waiting until you can figure it all out because you may miss a divine moment. Step out in faith and make sure your faith is in God, not in your own abilities. Let me be clear. When I say, "step out," I am not encouraging you to be presumptuous. Remember, God had already placed this vision of a book on my heart and I believed He was calling me into action. Never get ahead of God unless you want to be left holding the debt. Step out when He clearly has called you to action.

The weekend finally arrived when I intended to send my final manuscript to Kim, along with the agreed initial payment to jump-start the process.

As I tried to wrap up my writing, something felt as if it was missing. I did not have the right closing story to punctuate the importance of this project or to highlight God's glorious place in my ongoing story.

I was not quite sure what I was waiting for. I just knew I had to wait. God had hit the pause button for a reason that was about to become crystal clear.

Last night, I returned home around 1:00am from a powerful time of praying and conversing with a group of pastors. Regardless of the time of day, I hold fast to my homecoming ritual of bringing in the mail. At first, I thought I was holding a piece of junk mail. Prompted to take a closer look before tossing it into the trash bin, I noticed that familiar logo. It was correspondence from the IRS. I held my breath and opened the envelope that almost became trash. Having only received requests for payments or confirmation of having received a debt payment, I could not imagine what awaited inside.

I did a late-night double take because it has been years since I saw one of those—refund check appeared out of nowhere! I marveled that I now had more than enough money to get this book into print.

This closing story is a testimony to the provision of God, so that made it feel like a perfect way to sign off. Remember, I am no one special, but Jesus is. What you have witnessed Him doing in and through my life, He wants to do for you and through you. Please do not fall into the trap of expecting the exact same miracles or provision. We are each unique sons and daughters with diverse gifts, needs, and assignments from Heaven. What He chooses to do in your life may cause my story to pale by comparison. His plan for our lives is so much better than anything we could ever come up with on our own.

I hope that these real-life experiences have awakened a hunger and a level of faith that leaves you pursuing Jesus in a deeper way. I also trust that you will come away, regardless of your level of faith, ready to surrender all that you are and all that you have into the capable hands of our ultimate Father. He holds more vision and more resources in trust for your life than you could ever imagine. I am thankful that He continues to use my daily life to remind me that He is going with me. He is faithful and trustworthy with every aspect of my life. Once again, holding that refund check in my hands, I found myself proclaiming out loud:

You can't make this up—but Jesus can!

EPILOGUE

I truly hope you enjoyed reading this book. The stories of my life have all been scripted by Jesus by the power of His Holy Spirit. All I did was walk it out and write it down, hence, like I always say, *You can't make this up–but Jesus can.*

Hopefully, there was some level of entertainment woven into the pages. Not in a worldly sense, but through Him, I have experienced true joy. I think that is part of what Jesus meant when He said He has come that we would have abundant life. Life with God is never boring or mediocre. This book is only a small portion of the moments now woven into my memory and walk of faith that serves to remind me that He is always going with me. I have chosen these stories to encourage your journey and bring faith into your life, while empowering you to always look to Him as your guide and friend.

CHRISTIAN'S STORY: Raw and Unedited

NOTE FROM THE AUTHOR:

I felt compelled to close with Christian's story in his own words.

There are lots of young people with stories like the one you are about to read. Kids from troubled homes who don't have a good start in life who then struggle to catch up. When anyone is hurt at a young age, it can take years to recover. Who will show them the way?

I included this story not to put anyone down. We all make our own mistakes. I know the answer to what plagues individuals, families, towns, and cities as well as this country. It's Jesus, simply Jesus. I know what a difference Jesus has made in my life. That is why I chose to share the stories that make up this book.

As the book comes to completion, life goes on. I witness the difference Jesus is making every day in Christian's life.

I wrote this book because of the difference Jesus can make in your life. I hope this final story will draw you even closer to Jesus, and to those He has called you to love and influence.

For starters where to begin, my name is Christian and I'm a young white American born and raised pretty much in North Carolina. I'm 19 years old on this very day of April 26th, 2020 Sunday. I'm currently sitting in the Buncombe County Detention Facility. Yes, that's right! Jail, for what you may ask and why? Well that's to be told further on, I'd like to start off this story with where it all began. I was just a baby really, I was 4-5 living with my dad and stepmom in Georgia somewhere and life was, well what it would be for any ordinary kid at my age. But for me not at all, see my dad's name is Jason and my step mom was Molly and I had a little brother named Nick and then my dad and Molly had a kid named Adian (which I don't know him to this day.) Molly didn't really like me or my brother because we weren't her kids and my dad wasn't home, he traveled a lot due to work and well he was cheating on her. So, we were left with her a lot and when she was at work we had a nanny, which from what I can sort of remember she was sweet to us. Well see Molly started to abuse me and my brother but mostly me and thing you just wouldn't do to a kid at that age. Beats me for off the wall things that any kid at that age would do because they didn't know any better. Eventually our nanny found out and called DSS and they came and took me and my brother away and our mom came and got us.

My mom's name is Nicole. She was off doing her own thing and we were with her and our soon to be baby sisters dad. His name was Jeff. He was a great man from what I can remember, but my mom didn't keep the relationship going good for them. But that's none of my business to really tell.

Me and my brother went to live with our grandpa. And his name is Richard and our Aunt Ashley. Oh boy I can tell you all wonderful things about living with them and I can tell you bad. But I really loved my grandpa. I was a grandpa's boy growing up and boy when I tell you that man worked his butt off to get by in life he sure did. We never had much, but he always managed to somehow put food in our belly's and keep clothes on us and a roof over our head. Now later on to about the 6th grade was when I as a troubled little kid growing up took a jump into the deep end.

My brother was with my mom already at this point and he was living with her and her new husband who had just got out of prison about 2-3 years before they met. I stayed with them when they first met back in the 3rd grade for a couple of months and it was okay for a little while. But about mid-year of 6th grade I moved back with my mom and her husband "Slade" (was his name) and my little brother which by the way he is a year younger than me. So, I moved to Brevard, North Carolina from Swannanoa North Carolina which is about an hour away. I honestly had wished I never left my grandpas, but at the same time maybe it was for the best I don' know. But I moved in with my mom and it was okay for a little while till I met the wrong crowd of kids and started down a bad road of violence, drugs and stealing stuff. I was always away from home, never up to no good. That I can tell you much. Well 7th grade came along and I was smoking weed, dipping and getting in trouble. Well of course I wanted to be "hard" and "cool" like everyone else, so I started selling drugs and took some weed to school to sell. I sold it to this girl in front of a teacher who told on me and I got in major trouble. I got put on probation as a juvenile for about 2-5 years for distribution with intent to sell on school property. Well I was in and out of therapy and DSS because of my stepmom situations, and when this happened with probation it kind of made things harder on me and the house. My stepdad was a drug addict and got my mom hooked on pills, crack and heroin which made her a different woman. He was one sorry soul of a man. I can say that much. He abused my mom physically, mentally and verbally and just wasn't a true husband to her.

Well later I violated probation and was sent to a group home called Eliada. I was in the Lyons cottage all male level four lockdown facility. I was there for about 9-11 months and it was a pretty bad experience for me being my first time away from home and having my freedom taken away from me. But other than that, I got to learn how to ride dirt bikes, horses, take care of animals and work out. I also had a lovely therapist there named Mrs. Jane and I still have contact with her!

After all that time spent there I finally came

home and was off probation at this point. I went right back to being bad and hanging with the same people. Well sooner or later we moved again, but this time four hours away to a place called Aberdeen North Carolina and I started ninth grade high school there at Pinecrest high school. It was a real experience for me because I was involved in fights, drugs, having sex with girls, and chilling with gangbangers. I started skipping classes then school to go smoke weed and hang with the wrong group of kids like I did before. I was in the Air Force JROTC and I liked it, but I was failing the book work, which was more important. So, I was dropped from the class the next semester. Then I started to get into fights, skipping classes and my grades were terrible. Well this was the usual thing for me. I never paid attention in school so I ended up failing the ninth grade.

But I ended up trying to commit suicide and my mom found out and took me to the hospital and had me committed. This was the first time I've ever really attempted it. I could've never woken up again, but God was sure watching over me. I took 80 triple C's cough, cold, congestion which ended up making me so high it felt as if I was in my own matrix. So I was sent off to old vineyard mental hospital for about a week and talked to doctors, therapists and all for that week it was really all over school and my lousy stepdads and why I tried to die. I was being bullied at school then at home and I didn't feel like living.

But once I left the hospital I wanted to live back with my aunt and grandpa, but in Fairview North Carolina. And I started school at an alternative school called Community High school in Swannanoa North Carolina. I had to redo ninth grade again. I was doing good for a little while until I started making friends like I always did. It turns out I found myself in the wrong group again with no good influences in my group of friends. I started back smoking weed and hanging out with some older kids around town. Getting into nothing but trouble. Drinking, popping pills, and just excusing my language effed up and not thinking about anything else. I started selling weed, cocaine, Xanax, perks and more. Life seemed cool to me doing all of that. But that wasn't it, I was doomed to a path in life of sin and darkness. I just was too blind to see it. I was stealing from stores, cars, houses and even my own family. Getting high to impress my friends. But little did I know they were just using me for money and to do their evil deeds. I was always a fool to peer in group pressure. I never really stuck up for myself, and always let people push me around. My life wasn't really all I thought it was and made it seem to be. I started to hang out with people that were way older than me like 4-5 years older and drug dealers. I was partying and skipping school once again but not as much. Until I started getting suspended from school every day. I started car hopping and playing with guns. Thank God I didn't own my own gun though. I was 15 at this point turning 16. I started hanging with two well-known twin sisters named Sierra and Crystal. Crystal was a lesbian; they took me in as their family and I love them like my sisters dearly. I was always hanging out with them all summer every summer for a couple good years. Well they had a cousin named Cassidy and oh my she was just the most beautiful soul I've ever seen. A tan skin little hippie girl and she had a best friend named Destiny. Cassidy was about a year or two older than me. But I lied to her and told her we were the same age. Boy it was like love at first sight for me when I first met her. Now see I met her going to a church down the street from her house and while the twins live next to her so what a coincidence it was about the time I met her face-to-face, when I went to hang out with the twins one day after church. Now I never went to church to do good. I'd go to smoke weed with friends that went to the church also. That's also where I met my cousin Elijah a.k.a. biscuit.

Well I started spending a lot of time hanging around the twins because they were my people and plus, I like Cassidy, but she didn't feel the same about me. She just got out of a relationship with an older boy named Don and he broke her heart, but she was still in love with him. Well I can't express to you how much I cared for her and I had only known her for such a short period of time, but it felt like forever. This was my first real kind of love. She just never felt the same way about me. Well I'd buy her things she needed because I wanted to, I can't say how much money I spent on that girl. I never looked at her with lustful eyes either, I just wanted her for her. Soon enough she started to break my heart. I was with her and Crystal's girlfriend Ella out late one night skinny-dipping. I wouldn't get in the water because I can't swim and for sure I was insecure about my naked body. But for some reason all of us were drunk at this point I was sitting all alone on a log drunk and depressed. Well she walked up to me naked and when I realized I turned away and waited for her to put clothes on. Well we talked and I guess she just wasn't into the respect I had for her as a woman. She wanted a bad boy type of guy that had no respect for her body or her as a woman. Well we went back to Ella's house to hang out and get more drunk and well that's when I truly became an alcoholic at a young age which at 16 wasn't good at all. Well I started to get jealous of Ella being hugged up on Courtney, so I started to raise cain outside and the cops got called. I was so intoxicated and going crazy the neighbor came out and told me to shut up, so I cussed him out and he threw his dog down the hill. I was very out of my mind at that moment.

The cops showed up and took me home. Well I threw up all in the backseat of the cop car and all over the cops! My grandpa doesn't like alcohol, so you can be sure he was irritated beyond belief. It was 3 AM in the morning. I didn't talk to Ellen or Cassidy for a week or so! Neither of them was really happy with me, but who could blame them.

Well a while later I ended up stealing my aunt's car at nighttime and went and picked up one of my so-called friends and we drove all around town up to no good. We broke into a school shed and stole all sorts of tools and supplies. I pulled in a little too late and my grandpa woke up ready for work and walked out and saw the car in the middle of the road and went upstairs and found out I had snuck out my window. At this point I was hiding in the bushes. Well long story short they were very mad.

I ended up catching a train in Atlanta Georgia to Louisiana to live with my dad for the first time since I was a baby. I was 16. I stayed with him for about six months and honestly it was one hell of an experience. I ended up living with my aunt Leah and cousin Kallie in Picayune Mississippi and went to the Picayune Memorial high school for the time being. I absolutely loved getting to be around my cousin Kallie and her big brother Caleb and aunt Leah. I hadn't seen them in so many years since we were little kids. I got to hang out and do lots of fun things with Caleb, and I met new friends, but I only hung out with one dude and he was my homey. He wasn't as bad an influence as my friends from the past, but he wasn't all that good either. My first two weeks at the school I got into a fight and was suspended. I remember the boy's name Plank and he snuck up from behind me. I ended up going back to school and was dealing with problems at the house, because the one bad thing about my aunt Leah was she was a major alcoholic and drug addict, but she stopped doing drugs and stuck to alcohol and pills.

My cousin Caleb was on probation and hooked on dope which I hated for him. He had ended up going to prison for about 2 to 3 years when looking at 7 to 10 years and he always told me to stay out of trouble, that this life ain't for me and boy was he right. I ended up stealing my aunt Leah's pills and getting others and selling to make money.

Sooner or later I had to catch a train back to my aunt Ashley's house in North Carolina because of problems with my aunt Leah and my dad. I honestly wish I hadn't moved back because things got worse for me. I was getting in trouble more and just out of control. Well I moved back and started hanging with the same people again and doing the same stuff I was doing before. I tried to stay away but it was easier said than done! I met this girl from the hood named Shiame (black girl) And we started talking then dating and I started back with some cocaine and got bad on it. We dated for about 6 to 8 months and it wasn't all that bad besides the drug part.

Well I was in a program for school and Elida called ESTA and the program was run by a guy named Ted and a lady named Yvonne and it was a program to help us teens get good paying jobs and careers and how to handle finances and help us get places to live. I was in it for about two years. It helped me a lot. I had a job at the Renaissance Hotel as an internship in Maintenance. The funny thing is I met my great grandma that worked there. Then I switched over to Biltmore and worked in engineering at Deer Park Inn for a while. I honestly really liked doing work like that because I like working with my hands. Then I left Deer Park Inn and worked at the Eliada in their maintenance for about a month. I got to drive a golf cart around!

I left Esta for a bit because I started to get in more trouble. Then I met my so-called best friend Zay and he was a blood so that wasn't really a good influence in my life. I've known him for about two years now almost 3. We would smoke lots of weed, get drunk and pop bars. We started hanging out so much I was getting suspended from school every day and when I'd be able to go back, I'd make it a couple of hours a day or two before getting suspended again. Zay dropped out so he didn't help me at all.

I started dating this girl named Haley and at that time I've been put back on probation for disorderly conduct which was for getting on my brother's middle school bus and threatening a middle school kid for making fun of my aunt Ashley's weight. Because she was on the bigger side. The bus driver told me to get off and I refused to get off, so we got into a fight. Well that just made my life wonderful! Not really!

Well I got put on probation and was still smoking and doing bad crap. Well I soon had to go back to Eliada for 30 days. I went to the same cottage, but everything has changed dramatically! It wasn't the same group home when I had last been there when I was 12 or 13, now I'm 17. But I had been with Haley for 2 to 3 months and was there for a graduation and everything.

Well I then met a Cuban girl at Eliada my age named Christina and when I left after the 30 days I kept in contact with her.

During my time there for those days, Ted at ESTA was close with me and started taking me out to church with him at a place called the red rhino off Tunnel Road downtown Asheville. I met all the wonderful people that went there. See it wasn't a regular church, it was like a family get together of a group of people who are loved and worshiped God and Christ Jesus our Lord and Savior! There were about 20 to maybe 25 people and they were all different like me. And that's when I met Peter Blackshaw! What a wonderful man he turned out to be. I was in Eliada and he didn't even know me but for a week or so and started to come visit me there. We had wonderful conversations, and once about my life history and even what I always wanted to be growing up. To be an engineer designer for the military. But that soon faded away! Hope things got better, and I was released on my 27th day out of 30 in because I asked Pete to pray that I would. I felt like my request was answered by God because of him! Well I went back to my aunt's house and back to the usual things I did before! I started back hanging out with say and his brothers, I almost got down with G D's which is a gang. But I didn't and I'm thankful to this day I didn't. All this time started back I ended up doing terrible things, robbing people, and breaking into churches to steal donations. Yes, I said the donations. I was badly influenced by my friends.

But sooner or later I ended up getting in even more trouble at school, so I dropped out of school which was the dumbest decision I ever made besides being in jail! I was violating probation for it.

Pete was in my life and wasn't going anywhere. God told him strictly and clearly to take care of me and never give up on me no matter what. Because God has special plans for me but honestly, I couldn't see it. So, through a lot of it Pete stuck by me.

I ended up crossing the last line with my aunt and grandpa because I decided to steal my grandpa's car this time to go and see some girls. Stupid right? Well I ended up getting tired and Zay drove. He went off the road and popped the front tire on the car which scared me bad. Grandpa was madder than I had ever seen him in my whole life. I don't know why I did the things that I did hurt my family, but I did. I regret it every day!

My mom had come and got me and I went to stay with her and her friend Tim, little did I know he was an old perv trying to get laid by mom so he was going the extra mile to do so, future reference he never did LOL! But I ended up living there and paying rent because my mom left and was staying with her new boyfriend, she just met which turned out to be a crackhead creep!

Well I got a job with a friend at the Crowne Plaza Hotel resort doing landscaping on the golf course! I liked it! Also I got my first car thanks to Pete! He gave me a 1999 jeep Cherokee Sport five speed stick shift. He taught me how to drive it. He also helped me out with my rent later on because my mom wrecked my Jeep about a month or two later. The day I got off of probation and she wrecked it! I wasn't mad but disappointed really!

Well time went by and I was dating Christina and I cheated on her, so we broke up. Then I met up with a girl that went to Western Carolina University and I started talking to her. She was gorgeous. Her name was Stephanie and she was 19 and I was 17. I would go to work then go party, smoke weed, do acid and all sorts of wild stuff. Always blowing my money on unnecessary things I didn't need instead of paying for what I really needed. But at this point I was driving a moped to work which Pete bought me. And I started going to see Stephanie and of course Pete took me! Every time every weekend pretty much. I was living the teenage dream you could say! Me and Stephanie dated for about a month or two and then she broke up with me! I was still partying doing dumb things.

I quit my job at the hotel and ended up being out of a place to live. After I got my learners permit and was going to get my GED, but I quit the GED too. Well Pete ended up telling me I could move in with him rent free and I was like no way! So that happened and I ended up working for him, while he left his job to start landscaping/maintenance business. Time went by and he bought me a car /Subaru and I drove it like crazy! I started hanging out in that crowd again! Wasn't such a good idea if you ask me. I stopped caring for my responsibilities. I had to do which was insurance and all these court bills I had to pay because of speeding tickets, no seatbelt weed charges and more! If it wasn't Pete paying for them all pretty much, I'd be in jail right now. Well I mean back then! So, I ended up disrespecting his house rules and sleeping with women in his house. Lord forgive me for it.

I kept heading down a bad path but this time worse than ever! I was just robbing people every day and using people so bad I got to the point I found myself using Pete. I've never thought I'd end up doing that, but sadly I did and I regretted it every day. He still hasn't given up on me to this day after all I've done!

Well I met a girl named Lola and she was sweet and all but of course hanging around say, all I had in mind with her was sex, and then it turned to sex and then money, because she started to give me $100 and $300 and $600 and $1000. Whatever I asked her for she gave it to me, and she thought I loved her but I didn't. I started selling weed again. It was moving about a quarter pound a day or two thanks to her. I was driving around getting drunk and messed up off bars all day every day. Still robbing people too, but for the thrill and fun of it. It didn't matter if it was for $100, we did it just because we were bored.

Well sooner or later things started to catch

up with me and I started getting in shootouts, drive-bys and big fights. And the funny thing is Pete knew the whole time what I was doing, and he still stuck by waiting for God to save me! I started working at the ski lodge for the winter and it was cool, but then the season was over. I was back at landscaping and boy did I bust my butt off doing it! It was mostly me and just Pete for the most part, But then I bought a buddy of mine with me and he worked with us for a while! Well that ruined our friendship, he quit, and I lost a really good friend a true friend of mine. His name is Kevin. I'll tell you one thing that boy could bust his butt working in sure keep up with me for his size. But I always gave him too much heck and was too controlling. And I regret ever bringing them on because it ended our friendship.

Ended up going with Pete on a trip to New York City to visit his daughter and work on a boat he had bought a while back. Keep in mind this was my first time ever going to New York and boy was it amazing! I flew on a plane which was my first time also. And of course, again Pete paid for it all. I had about $400-$500 of my own money but he still paid for the plane ticket and all. But we got there and got our rental truck which was a blue Tacoma Toyota! And we listened to blue Tacoma California the entire trip when we were there. It was wonderful. Well I ended up experiencing a lot I have never seen before. Places I've never seen, ate food I've never eaten. We were there for probably a week or so when I got to Walk on the beach in Manhattan,

New York which I had never been to before. We worked on his boat, installed the new motor, and washed it down. I got to go on the water which I've never been on a boat in the ocean before and we sailed from the top of Montauk point to Sayville and boy I got so sunburned I was redder than a lobster. I got sun poisoning and I had to go to the hospital because my feet swelled up. We were on the ocean for about 2 to 3 days. I got to deep sea fish, something I've always wanted to do. We had finally come back, and I wasn't able to go back to work yet.

Then my dad came back into my life and he drove from Texas to North Carolina and stayed with me and Pete for a little while and I lost my cool.

Then when I started to get better, I met a girl named Diamond and oh boy did I fall in love with her. I was crazy over her and she was me too! We started dating immediately which wasn't a smart idea at all because she had just gotten out of a relationship and had been a while since I had been in one. I was still talking to a bunch of other girls. At this point she had graduated with no driver's license and I was a drop out with a driver's license, so it was a weird mixture for a relationship. I ended up messing up my Subaru, and Pete bought me a 1995 Jeep Wrangler five speed four-wheel-drive drop top and boy do I love that Jeep! Me and Diamond dated on and off for about 6 to 7 months, we cheated on each other, had major fights. She ended up moving in with me and Pete because I was driving to see her every day which she lived an hour and a half away. Well her moving in with me wasn't really a good idea either. We were always getting into arguments, fights and just wasn't good at all! Pete put up with it somehow! I ended up letting another friend of mine come work with me but that was a huge mistake because he was lazy and just complained 24/7. Well that friendship didn't last very long, and he didn't work with me either.

Diamond broke up with me and went back home and slept with her ex that she said she hated a lot. I was confused and crazy, but it happened. We ended up getting back together and she was addicted to cocaine and bars. When we met but I stopped doing all that before we met. So, it was hard for me. Especially with her being an outraged alcoholic like her mother. I ended up doing the craziest things I've ever done in my entire life and because of her while she was in a dark path and I tried my best to help her but ended up bringing myself down to my old self and ways again. And well let's just say she really brought out the evil, bad and good person in me. I want to change so bad she made me want to sell drugs, kill people, steal cars, and run with gangbangers. Because that was the lifestyle she was into. I was just stupid for getting into a relationship with her at if I'm being honest. Well things ended up getting worse because no matter what I did or how much money I spent on her she was never really happy, so I started to lose interest in a relationship and started to really cheat on her and not even care anymore about us· Because all she wanted to do was party and get drunk like I used to do· I stop doing all that because it gets old on me for some reason· I didn't like to do it anymore· Well I thought we were doing good when one night she was getting drunk and I left to go get her food and get gas in my jeep· I had a little gun and I robbed someone for 30 bucks· I was gone an hour or less· I got back and she was gone, she lied she said she got picked up by her friend and would be back· Well this turns out she left with another dude· I got mad and decided to get drunk for the first time in a while· I started to go crazy· I was standing outside waiting in the dark of the night for her to pull up· Plotting to do evil· The devil sure had my mind that night! They pulled up and I tried to open the guy's door and he pulled off with her still in the car· Without thinking I started busting shots at the car· Pow Pow Pow! Thank God it wasn't a big enough gun to go through the car or I would've... Well you know·

God surely was in my favor more than once or just a few times now I surely would have been in major trouble but there wasn't any proof of things I did, God wouldn't let there be, I don't know why·   I tried to kill myself over her, I was just sent to Linnon memorial hospital for a week and I was found a new person, let me explain· I found a purpose to live for, to help people forget! I got out and was strong, but I let her back in and I lost my head again sadly· Well that relationship was doomed from day one when we got together· One night when I was taking her back because she had moved back· She was drinking and started saying hateful things and I tried to grab a drink to throw it out and it spilled in her lap so she poured it all over me in my lap On my phone and all. Then she about killed me by taking off in my truck with my hand in the door handle standing outside. Well that relationship went south. I was hanging out, stealing cars, breaking into things, and was messing around with guns again. So long story short I'm here in jail because I continued to hang out with him and other bad people. I'm now 19, which I turned while in jail, I've been in here three months and I have a $185,000 bond with 11 felonies and 3 misdemeanors, I don't know how or what consequences I'm looking at. I've been getting closer to God and Jesus Christ, but the battle of afflictions is very strong.

I hope one day I will witness God using my story to change the world. That is why I chose to share this part of my journey.

Chris

Made in the USA
Columbia, SC
31 July 2023

21074168R00148